COLUMBIA GORGE
HIKES

Don and Roberta Lowe

COLUMBIA GORGE HIKES

Don and Roberta Lowe

A *Frank*
mato
PORTLAND

About the Authors

Don and Roberta Lowe have co-authored 14 hiking guides for Oregon, California, Colorado and southern Washington and one of mountain bicycling routes. Don's photos have been featured exclusively in two large–format books.

◆

Published in 2000 by
Frank Amato Publications, Inc.
PO Box 82112 • Portland, Oregon 97282 • (503) 653-8108

Softbound ISBN: 1-57188-203-0 Softbound UPC: 0-66066-00417-8
Photography by Don Lowe
Book Design: Esther Appel
Photo Cover: Starvation Falls
Overleaf: West end of the Columbia River Gorge

Printed by Star Standard Industries in Singapore
1 3 5 7 9 10 8 6 4 2

Contents

Cliff below summit of Table Mountain with Mt. Hood in background.

Ponytail Falls.

Union Pacific engine and freight train.

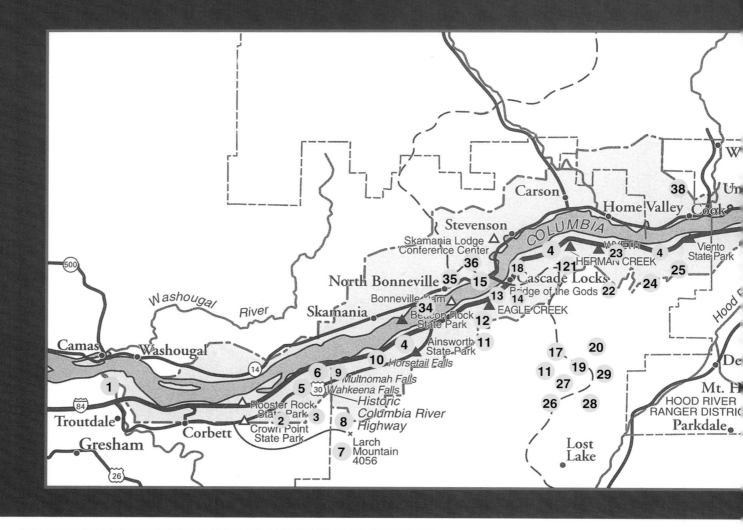

COLUMBIA GORGE HIKES

Hikers at Latourell Falls.

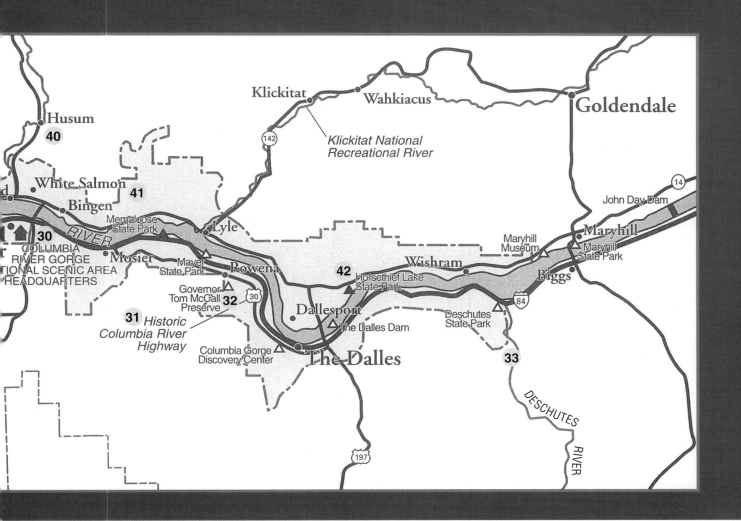

Upper Multnomah Falls.

Introduction

*I*f a person just drove the 80 some miles along the Oregon side of the Columbia River Gorge from the Sandy River to the Deschutes River—or the equivalent distance on the Washington side—and never once left his car he could not help but be awed by the steep walls, the plethora of waterfalls each with its own personality, and the dramatic changes in the vegetation and landscape between the western and eastern ends. When that visitor wanted a brief distraction from the generosity of Nature, he could amuse himself watching barge traffic on the Columbia River, trains snaking along either bank, or non-destination-driven sail boarders. And if that person got out of his car and walked just a few yards to some of the overlooks and informative markers, he would appreciate the geology and human history of the area even more. But, of course, the deepest way to savor this or any other outdoor area is to explore it on foot. And, as with that driver, Gorge trails afford the hiker many levels of enjoyment from easy strolls to demanding all-day loops and scenery that ranges from elegant forests, to impressive rock outcroppings to awesome panoramas. In moments of frustration, a hiker might even think, if just for a second, that the Gorge might offer too much because almost every trail on the Oregon side connects with several other routes and the number of combinations and permutations is, if not infinite, immense.

Summit of Indian Point.

Not only does the Gorge afford these scenic and hiking delights, but it offers the best of them when the higher mountain regions are closed by snow. The Gorge is particularly lovely in early spring because of the abundance of wildflowers. And in fall the maples, cottonwoods, vine maples, and dogwoods turn to yellows, golds,

Trail through field of balsamroot on upper Dog Mountain.

and reds. In winter, except during the worst of conditions when the Gorge definitely is not the place to be, frozen waterfalls and lower-elevation views no longer obscured by deciduous leaves lure visitors. And, although the hikes to summits with their far-ranging views should be reserved for clear days, the wooded areas can be just as attractive in cloudy weather as in sunny. Add some mist and those woods become other-worldly. And with an umbrella—or the rain gear of your choice—the woodsy trails continue to beckon in wet conditions.

This publication is first a picture book that attempts to capture the scenic variety of hiking in the Gorge and second a trail guide (and a mountain biking one for 11 of the routes). Therefore, the text is not as detailed as if the priority were reversed.

The first entry in the colored box indicates whether the trip is for hikers, backpackers, or bicyclists. With two exceptions, No. 29 and 40, the bike trips are never on trails but, rather, are on unpaved roads and the two sections of the

Historic Columbia River Highway that have been reopened as pedestrian/bike paths (Nos. 15 and 30), which also can be ridden with road bikes because they're paved. The only bike trip that is completely unsuitable for hiking is the one to Wasco Butte (No. 31). Although the Gorge trails, because of their proximity to the Portland-Vancouver area and their tendency to have considerable elevation gains, usually are done as day hikes, many can be made as backpacks. Definitely, backpacking is a way to combine the longer routes into loops that would be too much for most day hikers. Although it would involve a long car shuttle, one option for doing the long hikes that have their upper terminuses at roads (Nos. 7, 9, 17, 19 and 20) would be to have one party start at the top, the other at the bottom and exchange car keys when they meet. If you go any distance south on the Oregon side between Tanner and Starvation Creeks you will be in the former Columbia Wilderness, recently renamed the Mark O. Hatfield Wilderness. Permits are not needed for backpacking here.

The data for the next two entries in the colored box, distance and elevation gain, are for the entire trip, both out and back. All of the longer routes have excellent stopping points far short of their described destinations and mention is made in the text of especially good ones.

Metlako Falls.

The times the routes are open depend, of course, on weather conditions. During the winter months be very circumspect about venturing into the Gorge. The combination of cold temperatures and high winds can cause hypothermia. Those conditions, along with snow and ice, also make for treacherous driving and unsafe trails, especially those with any exposure. However, when the roads and lower routes are snow and ice free you can have much fine hiking.

From the box you can determine if the distance and elevation gain are what you want for that particular outing. However, to repeat, never let the long length of a trail discourage you from taking the route for as long as you have

the inclination or time. There is not one trail in the Gorge that isn't immediately meritorious.

The initial paragraph for each hike describes what is special about the hike and a few basic comments about the trail, such as if it's steep or has exposure. The second paragraph, "Variations", offers suggestions for side excursions, loop trips, car shuttles, and other options.

Driving directions are straightforward for almost all the trails because they begin from paved roads just off I-84 or Washington 14. Note that the numbers on the exits from I-84 indicate the mileage from downtown Portland. The only approach that is not paved is the rough two miles to the Tanner Butte Trail (No. 16) and the only complicated driving is to the four routes that begin from the saddle above Wahtum Lake (Nos. 26 through 29). The approach to these trips usually is from the Hood River Valley and unless you're very familiar with that area, you'll need to refer to an Oregon road map, the map for the Mt. Hood National Forest, or other road maps to find out how to reach Dee, from where the written directions begin. Once you leave

Wahkeena Falls.

9

Oregon 35, the Hood River Valley can be a confusing place through which to drive. However, it is also an exceptionally lovely area, so just enjoy the ride if you don't reach Dee on the first try.

Note that a trail park permit is required for most of the trailheads. After March 2000 the system will change somewhat in scope and cost, but the permits will continue to be available on a daily or annual basis from many commercial outlets and appropriate government agencies.

By no means is every route in the Gorge featured in this book. However, almost every one at least is mentioned at the appropriate place in the text. If you are only following the basic trail for each write-up, enough information is given that

Forest scene along the lower part of the Oneonta Trail.

you don't have to use a map. However, for most side trips that are suggested, you most likely will need to refer to one. But everyone, except the very infrequent and casual hiker, will (nay, should) want to have a map of the entire Gorge and be referring to it for every trip. If for no other reason, it's fun to see how the Gorge trails interconnect. Of course, there are several good reasons for studying maps and one is that by combining the text of any hiking guide with a map you'll enhance the content of both. Among the places you can obtain maps of the

Gorge are Powell's Travel Store at Pioneer Square in downtown Portland, Captains Nautical 138 NW 10th and Nature of the NW Information Center, 800 NE Oregon. Also, weekdays from 7:30 am to 4:30 p.m. maps and other Gorge-related publications are available at the office of the Columbia River Gorge National Recreation Area in Hood River. The addresses for it and the other agencies that administer trails in the Gorge are listed elsewhere in this book.

CAVEATS: Most of the Gorge trails are not child friendly, primarily because of exposure along many stretches. Among the exceptions are the pedestrian/bike paths along two sections of the Historic Columbia River Highway (Nos. 15 and 30). You as a parent will be the best judge of how appropriate any route is for your youngster

The most common reason people get into trouble while hiking and backpacking is because they grossly overestimate their level of experience and physical condition. Mention is made in the text if the routes are not official trails, if they are especially steep, etc. Ultimately, though, it is the hiker's responsibility to correctly evaluate his abilities.

As you read these words, during daylight hours people are working on trails and Nature 24 hours a day, in varying degrees, destroying them. In other words: Things Change. For good reason, texts like this are called guides, not gospels. Fine-tuning occurs on established routes and new routes are planned, particularly in the west end on the Washington side. Contact people at the Columbia Gorge National Recreation Area office for current information on these projects.

Tanner Butte and Mt. Hood from Tanner Ridge.

Some specific warnings that will remain consistent, regardless of a trail relocation here and a bridge out there.

Poison oak is encountered at some point along the lower elevations of most of the trails. Learn to recognize its various guises and avoid touching it. For people who are only mildly sensitive, dumping any clothing that may have come in contact with the plant in the washing machine and then taking a thorough shower should be enough. For the moderately sensitive, using a product like Tecnu on areas known to have touched a leaf is effective. If you include your dog on outings, be careful about hugging and petting him, because he's surely come in contact with the plant.

And just before you get in the shower, thoroughly check your body for ticks. Usually, they take their time about using you for a lunch counter but if one is, use tweezers to slowly and

Mountain bicyclists on the north end of Hamilton Ridge.

gently pull all of it out. The current medical advice is absolutely to consult a doctor if any redness or rash appears around the bite. Although the critters are most abundant in spring, check for them after any hike.

A more noticeable, but less serious, nuisance is mosquitoes. Fortunately, they are not a major annoyance in the Gorge, but you probably will encounter them on the Benson Plateau and a few other places. So, pack some repellent, just in case.

Make sure you have adequate water when you begin a hike because the days of being able to safely drink from a babbling

brook ended many decades ago. Backpackers will want to carry some sort of a purifying system. And, if you are backpacking, familiarize yourself with the rules for siting your camp and disposing of wastes.

None of the trips described in this guide involve potentially difficult fords. However, there are a few routes that are suggested as side trips or loops that do and mention is made if there is a ford. These crossings will be easier and safer if done late in the summer through early fall. One option for a ford is to carry tennis shoes and change into them. The next best choice is to take off your socks, so just your boots get wet. You could leave both your boots and socks on only if you're near the end of the hike, because usually walking a long distance with soggy socks guarantees blisters. Never cross in bare feet.

Small lake near the summit of Wasco Butte.

Even for what is supposed to be the shortest and easiest of hikes always have the attitude that you expect the best, but are prepared for the worst. Include in your pack extra clothing including hat, gloves and windbreaker, extra food, map of the area, whistle, and a flashlight. A compass isn't going to do you any good unless you know how to use it. However, if you are lost, reading the instructions would be one way to pass the time while you calmly wait for searchers to find you. Do not travel in the dark, unless you have a good flashlight. While on the subject of Do's and Don'ts, here are two of the latter that, unfortunately, only require a few people to cause obvious damage: Stay on the official trail—do not shortcut switchbacks; and do not pick wildflowers, leave them for others to appreciate.

If you are interested in helping preserve the Gorge for others to enjoy, one group you can contact is Friends of the Columbia Gorge at 522 S.W. 5th Ave., Suite 820, Portland, OR 97204, phone 503/241-3762.

Sandy River Delta

Sundown near the Sandy River delta.

1

HIKE/BIKE
DISTANCE: 0.5 to 6 miles
ELEVATION GAIN: 50 to 100 feet
HIGH POINT: 30 feet
ALLOW: 1/4 to 3 hours
OPEN: all year except during flooding and ice storms

The 1,400 acres of woods, wetlands, and fields immediately to the east of the Sandy River between I-84 and the Columbia River is crisscrossed by a web of old roads and paths that take you through groves of cottonwoods, along a sandy beach beside the Columbia River, across land once used for cattle grazing, past impressively immense mounds of blackberry bushes, and even beside a few lakes. If you venture as far as the Columbia River, you'll have views across to Washougal and up the Gorge, with Mt. Hood looming above Larch Mountain. On the Washington side, Silver Star Mountain and neighboring peaks fill a portion of the skyline.

This area is termed a "dispersed recreation site". In other words, you're pretty much on your own to explore where you wish. No signs tell you which way to go and, although an official trail system is being considered, now the only work being done is mowing routes through a few of those mountains of berry vines. The best times to visit are from late summer through winter because then you can travel where you want, not where the water level dictates. However, usually you can poke about the areas farther to the east most of the year. The unpaved roads especially lend themselves to exploring by bike. However, if you leave the roads, avoid riding over blackberry vines because you may end up with multiple flats.

Take I-84 to the Lewis and Clark Exit 18. If you're coming from the west, turn right at the end of the exit, go under the freeway and leave your car in the large, open area near the metal gate. People approaching from the east will come to the parking area immediately at the end of their exit.

As you explore the area keep yourself oriented and remember landmarks so at least you can backtrack if you were trying to make a loop that didn't come out where you had intended. The most straightforward route is to follow the road that heads east from the gate and soon comes to open, former pasture land and an old corral. Stay on the old bed and eventually take a path to a view of the Columbia River.

You can reach the "interior" by following one of the two roads that head north a short distance along the road that begins from the gate at the parking area. There is a connecting path between the more easterly of these two roads and the road described above that passes the corral.

You can gain quick access to the Sandy River by walking west along the paved road to where a path leads off the right side before you go under the freeway. You can parallel the Sandy River, following a meandering course of least resistance, to the Columbia River, walk east and then loop back to one of the roads that leads to your car.

Latourell Falls

Bracket fungus on downed tree trunk.

Hikers at Latourell Falls.

2

HIKE DISTANCE: 2.1 miles round trip
ELEVATION GAIN: 550 feet round trip
HIGH POINT: 750 feet
ALLOW: 1 1/2 hours round trip
USUALLY OPEN: February through December

Impressive Latourell Falls is the most westerly of the major cascades that visitors pass as they travel along the Historic Columbia River Highway. A pleasant little circuit goes above the main falls, travels along the east side of a narrow canyon, at its head passes the base of Upper Latourell Falls and then traverses out the west wall. To complete the loop, the trail descends along a circuitous route to near the base of the main waterfall before making the short climb to the starting point.

VARIATIONS: You can shorten the hike by just taking the trail down to the base of the main falls but, otherwise, this is a rarity for the Oregon side of the Gorge because there are no opportunities for side trips directly from the trail. However, there is a highly recommended little loop trail just 2.0 miles to the east along the Historic Highway. This circuit begins at Bridal Veil State Park and goes past overlooks above the Columbia River. You easily can see the wooden fences at them as you drive along I-84. In addition to the views, this area is particularly noted for the wildflowers it supports in the spring. Another path in the park goes down to a view of Bridal Veil Falls.

Approaching from the west, take I-84 to the Bridal Veil Exit 28 (not accessible to westbound traffic) and follow the exit road 0.2 mile to the junction with the Historic Highway. Turn right and head west 2.9 miles to the large parking area for Latourell Falls. If you're driving from the west on the Historic Highway, it is 2.5 miles east of Crown Point. Coming from the east, take I-84 to the Ainsworth Park Exit 35 and follow the Historic Highway west for 10.0 miles.

Follow the paved path up for 200 feet to a view of Latourell Falls, traverse along the east wall of the basin and make one set of switchbacks. Pass a closed trail and travel in and out of the canyon holding the upper falls. Pass the other end of that closed connector, which most likely never will be rebuilt. Climb past two overlooks and then descend to the Historic Highway.

You could cross the bridge to your starting point, but you're encouraged to extend the hike a bit by taking the trail that descends from near the west end of the span. At the bottom of the steps turn right and soon go under the bridge whose gracefully arched supports create the effect of a massive cathedral. Come to the pool at the base of the lower falls, cross a footbridge, and climb to the parking area.

Latourell Falls with autumn color.

Multnomah Basin

	BIKE
3	**DISTANCE:** 15 miles round trip **ELEVATION GAIN:** 2,800 feet round trip **HIGH POINT:** 2,150 feet **ALLOW:** 4 to 5 hours round trip **USUALLY OPEN:** March through November

Although the Multnomah Creek and Franklin Ridge Trails (No. 7) skirt Multnomah Basin, this mountain bike ride takes you along an old road through the heart of it. One portion of the Palmer Mill Road near the very beginning and a stretch on the west side of the Basin are steep enough that all but the strongest will have to walk, but by far most of the distance is along grades that are more fun than work to ride.

VARIATIONS: Highly recommended is the loop that returns on Larch Mountain and Brower Roads. You'd have an additional 9.6 miles and 500 feet of uphill, but six of those miles are fun downhill along a paved road.

From the west take I-84 to the Bridal Veil Exit 28 (not accessible to westbound traffic), drive the 0.2 mile to the junction with the Historic Columbia River Highway and park in the area between the two roads. If you're approaching from the west on the Historic Highway, this junction is 5.4 miles from Crown Point. Coming from the east on I-84 take the Ainsworth Park Exit 35 and continue west on the Historic Highway 7.1 miles.

Bike to the west along the Historic Highway for 0.1 mile to unpaved Palmer Mill Road on your left and take it for 1.9 miles to the junction of Brower Road, which you'll be returning on if you make the recommended loop. As noted above, portions of this lower section are steep and most cyclists will have to walk some of them. Turn left at the junction, go around a gate and travel beside Bridal Veil Creek. Stay on the main route where several side roads go to the left until the 5.6-mile point and then turn left onto a level road. This spur eventually curves to the right and becomes more rustic. The trail you pass on your left, which is closed to bicycles, connects with the Devils Rest Trail (No. 6). Come to a gate and go downhill on a rough surface. Cross Multnomah Creek on a bridge, bisect the Larch Mountain Trail, which also is closed to bicycles, and continue on the old road for about 1.3 miles as it follows a fun serpentine, but mostly level, course beneath deciduous trees across Multnomah Basin. Where you come to a turnaround in a grove of conifers, stop! Private property begins here, so don't go any farther.

To make the recommended loop, return to Palmer Mill Road and turn left. After 1.9 miles of a gentle mostly uphill grade come to paved Larch Mountain Road, turn right and have that nifty, long downhill for 5.9 miles to the junction of paved Brower Road. Turn right, have a few short uphills, 4.0 miles from Larch Mountain Road come to the end of the pavement and descend for 0.7 mile farther to the junction with Palmer Mill Road. An even longer loop, but with some additional

Road in Multnomah Basin under a thick cover of maple leaves in fall.

uphill, would be to continue on the Larch Mountain Road to its junction with the Historic Highway, turn right and follow the latter back to the starting point.

Gorge Trail No. 400

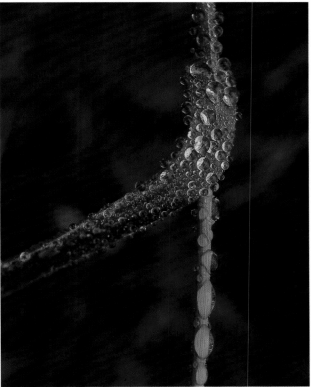

Water droplets on grass blade.

4

By combining existing routes and building new trails, a low elevation 35.5-mile traverse was created on the Oregon side of the Gorge between Bridal Veil and Wyeth. This Gorge Trail No. 400 has many, many access points and most of the elevation gains are modest, so doing one or more sections is an excellent choice when a hiker wants an easier outing, particularly if a car shuttle has been established. And, because of its elevation, Trail No. 400 provides hiking opportunities when the higher routes are still under snow.

Following completion of the most easterly portion, for several years in the '90s Trail No. 400 was open for its entirety. And then came the winter of '96-'97 and the flood of rocks that obliterated the 1.7-mile section between Dodson and Yeon State Park. Much of the devastation is obvious as you drive along the frontage road to Yeon State Park. Eventually this gap will be closed, but the new tread will be realigned to follow along the base of the cliffs so future floods would wash out only small segments of the trail.

The sections are described from west to east, but they all just as easily can be done the other direction. Note that Trail No. 400 itself does not always meet the access points at ends/beginnings given for the following sections. For example, if you were walking all the way from Cascade Locks to Wyeth you would not take the trail down to Herman Creek Campground. Also, note that for this one route mileages are given one-way only

When hikers use a car shuttle they will need driving directions for both ends as will people beginning from the east end of any section. To avoid repeating most driving directions twice, they are given below for the west end of each segment. The two exceptions for which mileages are given for the east ends are the last section and the one to the west of the part that is now buried under boulders.

Bridal Veil to Multnomah Falls

From the west drive on I-84 to the Bridal Veil Exit 28 (not accessible to westbound traffic) and in 0.2 mile come to the Historic Highway and park in the area between the two roads. Coming west along the Historic Highway, this junction is 5.4 miles from Crown Point. Approaching from the east, take I-84 to the Ainsworth Park Exit 35 and head west on the Historic Highway 7.1 miles.

Multnomah Falls to Ainsworth Interchange

Take I-84 to Multnomah Falls Exit 31. Walk through the tunnel to reach the trailhead. Or you can drive along the Historic Highway to Multnomah Falls.
East end: Take I-84 to the Ainsworth Park Exit 35. The signed trail begins from the south side of the interchange complex.

Yeon State Park to Tanner Creek

Approaching from the west, take I-84 to the Ainsworth Park Exit 35, at the end of the exit turn left and in 150 feet turn right onto the frontage road. Travel east on the frontage road 2.3 miles to the large parking area for Yeon State Park. Coming from the east, take I-84 to the Dodson-Warrendale Exit 37. After going under the freeway, turn left and proceed 0.4 mile to the parking area.

Tanner Creek to Eagle Creek

Take I-84 to the Bonneville Dam Exit 40 and go to the T-junction on the south side of the interchange. Stay right and descend to a parking area.

Eagle Creek to Cascade Locks

Approaching from the west, take I-84 to the Eagle Creek Recreation Area Exit 41, turn right at the end of the exit and park in front of the stone restrooms building. To return westbound, you first will need to travel east on I-84 to the Cascade Locks Exit 44. Coming from the east, drive to the Bonneville Dam Exit 40 and then head east to Eagle Creek Exit 41.

Cascade Locks to Herman Creek

Take the Cascade Locks Exit 44 from I-84 and at the far west end of the town follow the approach to the Bridge of the Gods. Leave your car in the park enclosed by the curve of the road before you actually reach the bridge.

Herman Creek to Wyeth

Approaching from the west, take I-84 to the Cascade Locks Exit 44 and continue east through the town about 0.9 mile to a fork. Take either one to Forest Lane on the south side of I-84. Turn left on Forest Lane and head east for 0.4 mile if you took the left fork or 1.8 miles for the right, passing the Oxbow Fish Hatchery, to the road up to Herman Creek Campground. If you're coming from the east take I-84 to the Forest Lane-Herman Creek Road Exit 47. Go under the freeway, turn right and head west 0.5 mile. Drive up the road to trailhead parking at the far west side of the campground area.
East end: Drive on I-84 to the Wyeth Exit 51 and at the T-junction on the south side of the interchange turn right. After 0.2 mile come to the entrance to Wyeth Campground and drive or walk, if the campground is closed, to the south, staying right where loops head left, another 0.2 mile to trailhead parking at the end of the road. Note that the road that continues west from the campground entrance connects with Forest Lane, where you can head eastbound on I-84 or continue west to Cascade Locks. This is a very scenic little drive and it's recommended that you follow it at some time.

Penstemon blooms and lichen on rock wall in Oneonta Gorge.

Bridal Veil to Multnomah Falls

4
DISTANCE: 7.9 miles one way
ELEVATION GAIN: 2,310 feet one way
HIGH POINT: 1,850 feet
ALLOW: 4 hours one way
USUALLY OPEN: March through mid-December

This most westerly portion, which climbs past Angels Rest and traverses east to Wahkeena Creek, originally was not going to be part of Trail No. 400, mostly because of the elevation gain. But it already was in existence and just too good to leave out. The first 2.3 miles of this route is the same as for hike No. 5.
VARIATION: You can make this section 2.0 miles shorter by taking the Wahkeena Trail (No. 6) down to the Historic Highway.
The trail heads east up the slope across from the parking area. Begin in lush woods and then cross a rocky slope. Pass a short spur on your left that goes to a view of Coopey Falls, cross Coopey Creek and wind up in woods. At 2.0 miles come to a more open rocky area and switchback up to a narrow crest. The trail to the left reaches the summit of Angels Rest in a few hundred yards.
To continue on Trail 400 turn right, walk along the narrow crest and reenter woods. The sometimes overgrown use path on the right eventually connects with one that returns to Trail No. 400 and in between has some routes branching off that inquisitive types might consider investigating. Have some uphill and at 2.8 miles cross a stream and pass a picnic area. Near 3.7 miles begin descending in six long switchbacks then climb slightly to Wahkeena Creek and travel near it for a few hundred feet to Wahkeena Springs, which appears with an impressive volume. The level spot below the trail here and

beside the stream is an excellent place for a snack stop. Two hundred yards along No. 400 from Wahkeena Springs come to the junction of the trail down Wahkeena Creek canyon to the Historic Highway.

If you're continuing to Multnomah Falls, stay right, climb for 0.4 mile and at a level area come to a connector down to the Wahkeena Creek Trail. Continue straight, pass the junction of the Devils Rest Trail (No. 6), and begin descending. At 6.9 miles come to the junction of the Multnomah Creek Trail (No. 7) that continues up to Larch Mountain. Turn left and follow down beside Multnomah Creek with its many cascades and falls. Pass the east end of the closed Perdition Trail, which connected with the Wahkeena Creek Trail just east of Wahkeena Falls. This troubled route was obliterated yet again during the winter of '96-'97. Eventually it will be rebuilt, but not in the near future. Immediately cross Multnomah Creek and come to the junction of the spur to the overlook at the top of Multnomah Falls. Stay right and climb on the paved trail to a crest and then begin winding down. The unpaved continuation of Trail 400 begins from the lowest switchback. The paved trail continues down to the Historic Highway at Multnomah Falls.

Forest scene.

Multnomah Falls to Ainsworth Interchange

4

DISTANCE: 5.5 miles one way
ELEVATION GAIN: 800 feet one way
HIGH POINT: 400 feet
ALLOW: 3 hours one way
USUALLY OPEN: most of the year

This section takes you through the cavern behind Ponytail Falls, the only formation like this in the Gorge that is visited by a trail.

VARIATION: You could add Triple Falls to your itinerary by making a side excursion that would add a total distance of 1.4 miles. This section of Trail No. 400 has several access points.

Follow the paved route up and across the bridge at Multnomah Falls and curve around to the north face of the slope. Unpaved Gorge Trail No. 400, identified by a plaque as the Ak-Wanee Trail, heads to the east from the first switchback. Near the east end of a swath of moss-covered rocks that supports some metal fencing you may be able to discern a path winding up the slope. This was the drolly named Elevator Shaft that went to Multnomah Basin and it would take a weird hiker, and one who is impervious to poison oak, to try it now.

At about 2.3 miles drop to the Historic Highway, walk along its shoulder for several yards and resume traveling on the trail, climbing for a bit and then leveling off. Pass beneath the remnants of an old rock wall just yards before the junction with the Oneonta Trail (No. 9). The trail to the left descends the short distance to the Historic Highway. To continue along Trail No. 400, stay right, climb and just before you curve into the canyon holding Oneonta Creek pass the west end of a path to a viewpoint on your left. It loops back to the main route a short distance farther. The open, rocky area is one of the several similar slopes along Trail No. 400 where you may hear a pika, also known as cony or rock rabbit.

Traverse to the junction of the Horsetail Falls Trail and, unless you plan to visit the view of Triple Falls, turn left and descend to the bridge across the narrow gorge of Oneonta Creek. Wind up out of the canyon and after a level stretch, where a path goes left to a viewpoint, go into the canyon holding Horsetail Creek and walk behind Ponytail Falls. The unsigned Rock of Ages use path that heads steeply up slope just before you curve out of the canyon climbs past an arch, comes to the Devils Backbone and then, with a somewhat more conventional tread, continues up to the Horsetail Creek Trail (refer to No. 9). Begin descending and at the third switchback stay straight on the continuation of Trail No. 400. Trail No. 438 (No. 10) continues down to the Historic Highway at Horsetail Falls.

A bit farther, if you look downslope, you'll see some old boards. These are the remnants of a fence that was built in the '20s to protect the railroad and Historic Highway from snow avalanches. At that time there was no forest cover here. Pass the upper ends of the westerly and easterly routes that go down to the highway at a restroom. The main trail continues traversing, passes two routes down to Ainsworth Campground and then meanders through woods before making several short switchbacks to the south side of the Ainsworth interchange.

Yeon State Park to Tanner Creek

DISTANCE: 3.8 miles one way
ELEVATION GAIN: 400 feet one way
HIGH POINT: 300 feet
ALLOW: 2 hours one way
USUALLY OPEN: most of the year

This section passes exquisite Elowah Falls and then traverses through pleasing woods, with one section along an overgrown road, before crossing Tanner Creek on one of the charming bridges of the original highway.

VARIATION: This section has no additional access points, but you do have the option of several short side trips, including one to Upper Elowah Falls (No. 12), another to Wahclella Falls (No. 14), the very steep use path to Munra Point (No. 13), and following the Nesmith Point Trail (No. 11) for a few tenths mile to a sobering look at one of the reasons why the section of Trail No. 400 immediately to the west doesn't exist any more.

Take the trail from the west side of the parking area at Yeon State Park, pass the start of the Nesmith Trail and travel under a long arch of deciduous trees. Climb through a stately coniferous forest to the junction of the spur to Upper Elowah Falls, stay left and a bit farther descend into McCord Creek canyon. Pass the base of Elowah Falls and cross the creek on a brand-new bridge. The immense boulder you skirt on the east bank used to be a viewpoint on the original trail 100 feet up slope. As you traverse out of the canyon you may be able to spot the end of this abandoned route.

Cross a more open area, then two swaths of rocks and 1.4 miles from McCord Creek cross Moffett Creek on another new bridge. One-tenth mile farther pass the use path to Munra Point and continue traversing the wooded slope. Travel on an old road bed, coming close to I-84 at one point, and staying left where spurs angle up to the right. Resume traveling on a trail and then descend along the west wall of Tanner Creek canyon to a section of the Historic Highway, now part of the Historic Columbia River Highway State Trail (No. 15). Turn right and in 200 yards cross the bridge over Tanner Creek.

Tanner Creek to Eagle Creek

DISTANCE: 2.9 miles one way
ELEVATION GAIN: 650 feet one way
HIGH POINT: 600 feet
ALLOW: 1 1/4 hours one way
USUALLY OPEN: most of the year

This segment climbs from the Bonneville Dam interchange, crosses the impressively rough road to the Tanner Butte Trail and then traverses to Eagle Creek. Note that the seemingly sturdy suspension bridge over Eagle Creek at the east end of this segment was destroyed by a slush flow—another victim of the winter of '96-'97—but its replacement is scheduled to be installed in 2000. You can contact the Columbia River Gorge National Scenic Area headquarters to learn if work is completed or, of course, you can drive to the Eagle Creek end of the segment and check the bridge's status in person.

VARIATION: You'll pass the 0.8 mile spur up to Wauna Viewpoint with its views down onto Bonneville Dam and you're encouraged to make this side trip. The short trail to Wahclella Falls (No. 14) begins from the west end of this section.

The signed trail starts from the T-junction at the south side of the interchange, climbs a bit and then follows a catwalk over a pipe. You can see the remains of the old flume that originally carried water to the fish hatchery. Continue up in woods and then stay left where you come to an old road, veer left again and follow it to Tanner Road. Turn left and follow it about 0.2 mile to where it makes a sharp curve to the left. The trail, which may not be signed, resumes from the southeast side of the curve.

Traverse for 0.5 mile to the junction of the recommended spur to Wauna Viewpoint, which gains 450 feet as it switchbacks up to the overlook. Trail No. 400 descends in two sets of turns, curves into Eagle Creek canyon and then crosses the bridge (assuming it has been rebuilt) over Eagle Creek. Turn left to reach the next section of Trail No. 400 or your car, if you've established a shuttle here.

Eagle Creek to Cascade Locks

DISTANCE: 2.7 miles one way
ELEVATION GAIN: 300 feet one way
HIGH POINT: 200 feet
ALLOW: 1 1/2 hours one way
USUALLY OPEN: most of the year

This route follows a section of the Historic Columbia River Highway State Trail (No. 15), the same route that Trail No. 400 was on just west of Tanner Creek. You'll travel through some woods not quite like any other in the Gorge and at the very end for a couple hundred feet you'll be on the most northern portion of the Pacific Crest Trail in Oregon.

VARIATIONS: From near the 2.0-mile point you could continue along the paved State Trail to Cascade Locks. You pass the lower end of the moderately steep Ruckel Creek Trail (No. 18) but, although it is an exceptionally scenic route, there is no specific destination suitable for a short side trip.

From the stone restroom building at Eagle Creek walk to the east along the road to the campground for about 75 yards to a signed trail that marks the route to Cascade Locks. Climb, parallel the north side of the campground to its east end and then drop to the paved State Trail. Turn right, pass the start of the Ruckel Creek Trail at the east side of the bridge over Ruckel Creek and 0.8 mile farther come to the resumption of Trail No. 400 a short distance before the paved road goes through a tunnel. Traverse through woods and across more open areas to a dirt road. Trail No. 400 (now part of the PCT) continues from the other side. However, to reach Cascade Locks, turn left, come to pavement, go under the freeway, veer left onto a trail and come to the park just before the Bridge of the Gods.

Cascade Locks to Herman Creek

4

DISTANCE: 6.0 miles one way
ELEVATION GAIN: 1,400 feet one way
HIGH POINT: 1,250 feet
ALLOW: 2 1/2 hours one way
USUALLY OPEN: February through December

Along all but the east end of this section you will be following the northernmost part of the Pacific Crest Trail in Oregon. The varied terrain includes woods with unique rock pinnacles, two large talus slopes, and an abundant salamander population.

VARIATIONS: You can make a 0.3-mile round-trip excursion to Dry Creek Falls, which is anything but. You'll pass the junctions of several major trails near the east end, but there are no specific points on them that would be suitable for a short side trip. Although, as always in the Gorge, there is attractive scenery, regardless of how far you go.

Take the signed path that begins opposite the restroom building on the south side of the access road to the Bridge of the Gods. In a short distance go under I-84 and turn right onto a road. Where the paved road curves left, continue in the same direction you were heading along the unpaved road for about 100 feet to Trail No. 400, which is concurrently the PCT, heading off on the left. At 0.9 mile come to a narrow dirt road, turn right and follow it for about 75 feet to the resumption of the trail on your left. Watch for those salamanders because they are interesting and, more importantly, because you don't want to step on any of them.

Come to a wide dirt road just before you cross the bridge over Dry Creek. If you want to make the side trip to the falls, turn right onto the road. At 3.8 miles come to the junction of the Herman Bridge Trail, where the PCT heads up to the Benson Plateau (No. 19). Stay

Tug and barge in the new Bonneville Dam lock from Wauna Viewpoint.

left, descend to the bridge over Herman Creek and climb to a junction where Trail No. 400 and several other routes head to the right. To reach the trailhead parking area, stay left, eventually cross a powerline access road and wind down in woods. Watch for a trail heading off to the right at one of the switchbacks and take it. If you miss the turn you will end up at the work center instead of the campground.

Herman Creek to Wyeth

4

DISTANCE: 5.4 miles one way
ELEVATION GAIN: 950 feet one way
HIGH POINT: 1,000 feet
ALLOW: 3 hours one way
USUALLY OPEN: mid-February through December

This is the most easterly and also the newest section of Trail No. 400. Both ends are in woods but the middle portion, with its drier, rocky, more open character has an almost alpine feel.

VARIATION: As with the previous section, the route passes the junctions of several major trails, but none has specific features that would be appropriate for a short side trip.

Climb from the parking area at Herman Creek Campground to a junction, turn left and make several switchbacks to a powerline access road. Cross it, follow up along another road for a few yards and begin traveling on a trail. After one set of short switchbacks come to a junction. The route to the right is the section of Trail No. 400 that heads west. However, to head east on Trail No. 400, stay left and in 200 yards meet an open area. From here climb along a dirt road and then level off. At 1.4 miles come to a flat, treeless area on your left. Trail No. 400 angles off from the northeast corner. The Gorton Creek Trail begins from the east side and the Nick Eaton (No. 21) and Herman Creek (No. 20) Trails begin a short distance farther along the road.

Meander on the level through woods to the rim and then traverse to the east along the forested slope. Have those more open stretches and near the end descend in deeper woods to a junction. The route that continues straight goes to North Lake (No. 22). Turn left and walk several hundred yards to the trailhead parking area.

Whimsical sign that once marked the now-overgrown Primrose Trail from Devils Rest.

Angels Rest

5

HIKE
DISTANCE: 4.6 miles round trip
ELEVATION GAIN: 1,450 feet round trip
HIGH POINT: 1,600 feet
ALLOW: 3 1/2 hours round trip
USUALLY OPEN: March through mid-December

Hikers on summit of Angels Rest.

Angels Rest is the most westerly viewpoint in the Gorge that is reached only by trail. From its broad, open summit hikers have superb views to the north, to the east and down river toward Portland. Angels Rest, unlike trips that go into side gorges, is not sheltered, so pack extra clothing if you make the hike in windy weather.

An uncommon feature of this trip is that part of it goes through a portion of the 1,430 acres between Multnomah Falls and Bridal Veil that were burned in early October, 1991. Interestingly, the visual results are more unattractive from I-84 than along the trails that go through the affected areas. Hikers focus, not on the snags, but on how regenerative plants can be and they also note, somewhat ruefully, that views have become more extensive in the burned areas. One of the major, insidious results of fires, however, is the damage, because of the loss of ground cover and healthy root systems, to the stability of the slopes, never all that great in the Gorge in any case. Sections of trails that already were marginal

Hikers on trail through burned area below summit of Angels Rest.

subsequently were affected even more severely by heavy rains, particularly those of the infamous winter of '96-'97.

VARIATIONS: By establishing a short car shuttle, hikers can make a one way trip by continuing east from Angels Rest on Gorge Trail No. 400 (No. 4) and returning along either the trail to Wahkeena or Multnomah Falls, with an optional side trip to Devils Rest (No. 6).

From the west drive on I-84 to the Bridal Veil Exit 28 (not accessible to westbound traffic), go 0.2 mile up to the junction with the Historic Highway and park in the area between the two roads. Coming from the west along the Historic Highway, this junction is 5.4 miles from Crown Point. Approaching from the east, take I-84 to the Ainsworth Park Exit 35 and head west on the Historic Highway 7.1 miles.

The trail begins across the Historic Highway from the parking area. After a short stretch through lush woods, traverse a rocky swath where you'll have your first views down onto the Columbia River and across to Cape Horn. Pass a short spur to a view of Coopey Falls and a bit farther cross Coopey Creek. Resume winding up through woods and at 2.0 miles come to an open rocky area. Switchback a final time and come to a possibly unsigned junction on a narrow crest. Trail No. 400 continues along the ridge top to the east (right) here and is the route of the optional extensions. To reach Angels Rest, turn left, have an easy scramble over some boulders and come to the big summit area. A little network of paths wends about to the west and south from the top.

"The Face" on the summit of Angels Rest.

Wahkeena Creek-Devils Rest-Multnomah Falls Loop

6

HIKE
DISTANCE: 8.3 miles round trip
ELEVATION GAIN: 2,500 feet round trip
HIGH POINT: 2,430 feet
ALLOW: 5 1/2 to 6 hours round trip
USUALLY OPEN: April through mid-December

In addition to visiting two of the most popular waterfalls in the Gorge—Wahkeena and Multnomah—the route passes Fairy Falls, arguably the prettiest, as well as Upper Multnomah Falls and many smaller cascades.

Wood sorrel.

VARIATIONS: You can shorten the hike by omitting the 1.6-mile spur to Devils Rest or you can create an even easier outing by making a little return loop off the Wahkeena Trail. For a longer variation you could establish a short car shuttle and combine poetically Angels Rest (Nos. 4 and 5) and Devils Rest.

If you're approaching from the west, you can either follow the Historic Highway 8.0 miles east from Crown Point to the parking area for Wahkeena Falls or take I-84 to the Bridal Veil Exit 28 (not accessible to westbound traffic) and then continue east along the Historic Highway 2.6 miles. If you're coming from the east, take I-84 to the Ainsworth Park Exit 35 and continue west on the Historic Highway for 4.5 miles.

Walk along the paved path that initially climbs to the west and eventually passes Wahkeena Falls. A short distance farther come to the junction of barricaded Perdition Trail, another casualty of the winter of '96-'97. Turn right and wind up in 10 switchbacks to a crest where a spur goes right to an overlook and the main trail heads left. Beyond Fairy Falls wind up to the junction of the Vista Point Trail, the lower end of the shorter return loop. Continue up to the junction of the section of Gorge Trail No. 400 that heads west to Angels Rest and in about 200 yards passes an excellent snack stop at Wahkeena Springs.

To continue the circuit, turn left and climb for 0.4 mile to the upper end of the Vista Point Trail, the possible shorter loop down to the Wahkeena Trail. Stay right and in 75 feet veer right onto the Devils Rest Trail.

Wind up in switchbacks and then have a level respite along the breaks where you can see ahead to Devils Rest. The trail off to the left goes to the road described in No. 3. Pass views of Mounts Rainier and Adams and several Gorge landmarks and continue meandering up to the wooded summit.

Retrace your route to the Wahkeena Trail and head east at a gentle downhill grade to the junction of the route along Multnomah Creek (No. 7). Turn left and hike parallel to the unremittingly attractive stream. Pass the closed east end of the Perdition Trail just before you cross Multnomah Creek and come to the spur to the overlook at the top of Multnomah Falls. Climb a short distance to the rim on the now-paved tread and then wind down, staying on the pavement where Trail No. 400 (No. 4) continues to the east, pass Multnomah Falls and come to the Historic Highway.

To complete the loop, walk west along the Historic Highway from the stone building for about 300 feet to a trail and follow it 0.5 mile back to your starting point.

Wahkeena Falls.

Wahkeena Falls in winter.

Multnomah Creek Trail to Larch Mountain

Upper Multnomah Creek.

HIKE

7

DISTANCE: 13.6 miles round trip
ELEVATION GAIN: 4,300 feet round trip
HIGH POINT: 4,056 feet
ALLOW: 7 hours round trip
USUALLY OPEN: late May through mid-November

From Sherrard Point at the edge of the sheer north face of Larch Mountain you'll understand why this landmark is so easy to identify from the west or east. Much of the route to the summit's 360-degree panorama is beside Multnomah Creek, definitely one of the most attractive streams in the Gorge.

VARIATIONS: You can make a perfect loop by taking the Franklin Ridge Trail back. It would involve 2.0 miles more and only slight additional uphill. With a short car shuttle you could return along the Oneonta Trail (No. 9) or follow Bell Creek Way to the Horsetail Creek Trail and then return either along the Nesmith Point Trail (No. 11) or the Oneonta Trail. With a longer shuttle, you could do the trip one way (refer to No. 8).

Take I-84 to the Multnomah Falls Exit 31, walk through a pedestrian tunnel and cross the Columbia River Historic Highway. You can also take the Historic Highway 3.2 miles east from its junction with the Bridal Veil Exit 28 (not accessible to westbound traffic) or 3.9 miles west from the Ainsworth Park Exit No. 35.

Follow the crowds to the high bridge in front of Multnomah Falls, traverse out of the canyon and begin winding up, at the first turn passing the junction of Trail 400 (No. 4). From the rim descend a short distance to the junction of the spur to the overlook at the top of the falls. Stay left on the unpaved tread, cross Multnomah Creek and in several yards stay left again at the junction of closed Perdition Trail. Travel beside Multnomah Creek, pass Upper Multnomah Falls

and stay left again at the junction of the Wahkeena Trail (No. 6) at 1.8 miles.

Recross Multnomah Creek on a high bridge and 0.4 mile farther come to the junction of the High and Low Water Trails. If you take the former, stay right at the path to Multnomah Basin. Two-tenths mile beyond where the two routes rejoin, cross Multnomah Basin Road (No. 3) and in 0.3 mile stay right at the junction of the Franklin Ridge Trail. Cross the East Fork of Multnomah Creek and then in 0.5 mile the main flow. Farther on, traverse a rocky slope and at 4.8 miles stay right at the junction of Multnomah Creek Way Trail (No. 8). At 5.3 miles pass a level area and cross a spur road coming in from Larch Mountain Road. Eventually, pass picnic sites and come to the parking area. Continue in the same direction you were heading to the other corner to take the paved path the 0.2 mile up to Sherrard Point.

The most straightforward way to make any of the recommended loops is to walk down the Larch Mountain Road about 0.4 mile to the upper end of the Oneonta Trail on your left. Descend for 0.9 mile and stay right at the junction of Multnomah Creek Way Trail (No. 8). In 0.9 mile come to the Bell Creek Trail on your right. The Oneonta Trail in 0.8 mile passes the junction of Multnomah Creek Spur Trail, which goes left to the Multnomah Creek Way Trail, and 0.7 mile farther comes to the junction of the Franklin Ridge Trail.

Upper Multnomah Falls.

Multnomah Creek Way-Larch Mountain Loop

8

HIKE
DISTANCE: 6 miles round trip (including side trip to Sherrard Point)
ELEVATION GAIN: 1,300 feet
HIGH POINT: 4,056 feet at Sherrard Point
ALLOW: 3 1/2 to 4 hours round trip
USUALLY OPEN: late May through mid-November

Because of its location, the overlook on Sherrard Point at the brink of Larch Mountain's sheer north face affords an uncommon perspective west down the Columbia River past the steam plumes at Camas, the Sam Jackson (I-205) Bridge, and beyond toward Portland. Additionally, the viewpoint provides far-ranging scenes in all other directions, including the major Cascade Peaks from Mt. Rainier south to, on an exceptionally clear day, the Three Sisters and east over landmarks in the Gorge to Mt. Defiance (No. 24), always easily identified by its tall towers.

VARIATIONS: You could make a slightly longer loop by taking the Oneonta Trail to its junction with the Multnomah Spur Trail and following the latter to the Multnomah Creek Way Trail. Note that the area to the northeast below Larch Mountain supports a tangle of trails and it is highly recommended that you have a map with you if you want to investigate them.

Take I-84 to the Corbett Exit 22 and climb steeply for 1.4 miles to the junction with the Columbia River Historic Highway. Turn left (east), after 2.1 miles come to the junction of the Larch Mountain Road, stay right and follow it the 14 miles to

Mt. Hood from Sherrard Point on the summit of Larch Mountain.

its end at a large parking area. If you're approaching from the east on the Historic Highway, the junction of Larch Mountain Road is 0.7 mile from Crown Point.

Walk back along the Larch Mountain Road for about 0.4 mile to a sign off the south shoulder that marks the upper end of the Oneonta Trail (No. 9) and follow it downhill for 0.9 mile to a junction. Turn left on Multnomah Creek Way Trail and follow an old logging railroad bed before resuming a more noticeable downhill grade on, for the Gorge, an unusually rooty and rocky tread. If you make the circuit later in

the summer, you can savor some huckleberries from the bushes that line the route. Travel parallel to a meadow and near its far end look for a path that goes several yards the edge of the clearing where you can look up to Sherrard Point.

Just before a bridge come to a junction where the Multnomah Spur Trail heads right and connects with the Oneonta Trail. Stay left, cross the bridge and begin climbing to the junction with the considerably smoother surfaced Larch Mountain Trail (No. 7). Turn left and continue up at a gentle grade to a level area

Meadow below summit of Larch Mountain.

where a shelter once stood. Cross a spur road that comes in from the Larch Mountain Road and farther on pass picnic sites just before you come to the northwest corner of the parking area.

To reach Sherrard Point, follow the paved trail from the northeast corner and then climb a flight of steps for the final distance to the fenced overlook. The path with steps to the left of the paved path at the parking area climbs past a picnic spot before descending back to the main route.

Sunset over the Columbia River from Sherrard Point on the summit of Larch Mountain.

Oneonta Trail

9

HIKE
DISTANCE: 16.2 miles round trip to Larch Mountain
ELEVATION GAIN: 4,600 feet round trip
HIGH POINT: 4,056 feet
ALLOW: 8 hours round trip
USUALLY OPEN: late May through early November

From 0.5 mile to 2.9 miles the Oneonta Trail travels through narrow Oneonta Creek canyon, early on passing Triple Falls. It then climbs over the ridge separating the Oneonta Creek and Multnomah Creek drainages and continues to Larch Mountain.

VARIATIONS: A good turnaround point for people wanting a shorter hike is at 2.9 miles beside Oneonta Creek. The elevation gain just to here is 1,500 feet. The trail could be done one way using a car shuttle (see No. 8). With considerably shorter shuttles, the Oneonta Trail can be combined with the Franklin Ridge or the Multnomah Creek (No. 7) Trails. A recommended, more demanding, option, which also involves a short car shuttle, is to take the Horsetail Creek Trail to the Nesmith Point Trail (No. 11) and return along that route. The total distance for this trip would be 13.9 miles with 4,200 feet of uphill. Because of the possibly

Forest scene along the lower part of the Oneonta Trail.

difficult ford of Oneonta Creek, this combination is best done from late summer through early fall.

Drive on the Historic Highway 5.2 miles east from its junction with the road up from the Bridal Veil Exit 28 off I-84 (not accessible to westbound traffic) or 1.9 miles west from the Ainsworth Park Exit 35 to a wide spot for parking on the north side of the road across from a sign identifying the Oneonta Trail. This trailhead is 0.6 mile west of Horsetail Falls.

The route that heads west from the first switchback is one section of Gorge Trail No. 400 (No. 4) and, until the next junction, you concurrently will be on it. Continue up, curve into Oneonta Creek canyon, and at 0.9 mile come the trail to Ponytail and Horsetail falls (No. 10) heading downhill. Stay right and at 1.6 miles pass Triple Falls and 0.1 mile farther cross Oneonta Creek. After 1.1 miles recross it, again on a bridge, and come to the junction of the Horsetail Creek Trail. To continue to Larch Mountain, turn right and mostly climb along a far more scenic realignment of the original tread to the junction with the Franklin Ridge Trail at 4.6 miles.

Turn left, in 0.5 mile stay left at the junction of Multnomah Creek Spur Trail, which connects with Multnomah Creek Way Trail, and 0.8 mile farther stay right at the upper end of Bell Creek Way, which connects with the Horsetail Creek Trail. After 0.9 mile stay left at the upper end of Multnomah Creek Way Trail, continue the final 0.9 mile to Larch Mountain Road, turn right and walk up the road 0.4 mile to the parking lot. Refer to No. 8 for details of the summit area.

The optional route along the Horsetail Creek Trail is straightforward: Pass the lower end of Bell Creek Way 2.3 miles from the ford and beyond the easy crossing of the three forks of Horsetail Creek stay right at the unsigned use path to Rock of Ages Ridge (see No. 4). Where you come to a road at 5.6 miles from Oneonta Creek, turn left and go the final 0.4 mile to Nesmith Point.

Oneonta Creek just before the top of Oneonta Falls.

Upper Oneonta Creek.

Horsetail Falls Oneonta Creek Loop

10

HIKE
DISTANCE: 2.7 miles round trip
ELEVATION GAIN: 500 feet round trip
HIGH POINT: 400 feet
ALLOW: 1 1/2 hours round trip
USUALLY OPEN: February through November

The highlight of this charming little loop is where the trail goes through a huge cavern behind Ponytail Falls. You'll also pass a viewpoint above the Columbia River and farther on be able to peer down into very narrow Oneonta Creek gorge. Note that this loop involves walking along the Historic Highway for 0.6 mile.

VARIATIONS: You could add a third waterfall by following the Oneonta Trail (No. 9) for 0.7 mile to Triple Falls and even continue up the canyon, if you wanted a longer hike. All but the ends of the loop you'll be taking are also part of Gorge Trail No. 400 (No. 4) and you could explore the segments of that route that head west and east.

From I-84 take the Ainsworth Park Exit 35 and head west on the Historic Highway 1.3 miles to the large parking area across from Horsetail Falls. Approaching from the west you could also take the Bridal Veil Exit 28 (not accessible to westbound traffic) and head east on the Historic Highway for 5.8 miles.

Head uphill from the big wooden trail sign and at the third switchback stay right where Trail No. 400 continues to the east. Make one more set of switchbacks and contour along the moss, fern, and wildflower-dotted rock face. The steep use path on your left just after

you curve into the canyon holding Ponytail Falls is an unofficial route that eventually connects with the Horsetail Creek Trail (see No. 9). The cavern behind Ponytail Falls was created by the erosion of a band of rock that is composed of less-resistant material than what is above and below it.

Beyond the west side of the canyon come to a fork where the right branch loops past a viewpoint, descend to the bridge over Oneonta Creek that is just upstream from the top of Oneonta Falls and then climb briefly to the junction with the Oneonta Trail. To reach Triple Falls turn left or, to complete the loop, turn right.

Climb gradually and traverse a rocky swath where you may spot or at least hear the bleat of a pika and then leave the canyon and descend to the junction of the section of Trail No. 400 that continues to the west. Turn right and descend to the Historic Highway. Head east along it for 0.2 mile to the lower end of Oneonta Gorge. In the past when the water level was at its lowest, people would pick their way along the stream bed to the base of Oneonta Falls. However, log jams have created extremely deep and very dangerous pools and access has been blocked. Continue along the highway another 0.4 mile to reach your starting point.

Oneonta Creek gorge.

Ponytail Falls in winter.

Ponytail Falls.

Nesmith Point

HIKE

11

DISTANCE: 9.8 miles round trip
ELEVATION GAIN: 3,810 feet round trip
HIGH POINT: 3,872 feet
ALLOW: 7 hours round trip
USUALLY OPEN: June through November

*T*rees now thoroughly block the once superb view from the site of the former fire lookout but just before the summit, hikers do have an intimidating view from the rim of the Gorge down onto Beacon Rock and beyond to Hamilton and Table Mountains (Nos. 34, 36, and 37) in Washington.

VARIATIONS: A satisfying stopping place is at 3.0 miles on the topmost rim of the two basins you wind through and that are unlike any others you visit in the Gorge. However, note that two-thirds of the elevation has been gained by this point. Two different loops involving car shuttles are possible. One is to return along the Horsetail Creek and Oneonta Trails (No. 9). The second is to combine the Nesmith Trail with the Moffett Creek Trail, which offers a very scenic variety of uncommon views and terrain. Because of the ford on each option, both are best done later in the summer. Also, if you do plan to follow the Moffett Creek Trail, it is recommended that you follow it up.

Approaching from the west, take I-84 to the Ainsworth Park Exit 35, at the end of the exit turn left, following the signs to Dodson and Warrendale and in 150 feet turn right onto a frontage road. Travel east 2.3 miles to the large parking area for Yeon State Park just before the frontage road rejoins the east bound lanes of the freeway. Coming from the east, take I-84 to the Dodson-Warrendale Exit 37. After going under the freeway turn left and proceed 0.4 mile to the parking area.

Follow the trail up from the west side of the parking lot, switchback and after 70 feet turn right. The route that continues east passes Elowah Falls (No. 12). Meander up in woods for 0.8 mile to a former junction at an immense washout, which was, until the winter of '96-'97, a section of Gorge Trail No. 400 (see No. 4). Continue up to the west edge of the lower basin and make a scenic tour of both bowls as you climb to the crest at 3.0 miles. Turn right and farther on begin

Upper portion of Nesmith Point Trail in fog.

traversing along the southwest facing slope. At 4.6 miles come to a junction, turn right, soon come to an old road bed, turn right again and follow it up to the summit.

If you're returning along the Horsetail Creek Trail, from the summit retrace your route down the road, pass the junction of the trail you took in and 0.1 mile farther turn right onto the trail.

If you're taking the Moffett Creek Trail in, follow the driving directions for Tanner Butte (No. 16) but continue beyond that trailhead to a gate. Walk along the road for 2.5 miles to the Tanner Cutoff and Tanner Creek Trails on your left and follow it. Stay right at the junction of Trail No. 448 and about 0.9 mile farther veer right onto the Moffett Creek Trail.

Ford Tanner Creek and begin winding up in one mile of switchbacks. Then begin traveling through ever-changing, but always attractive, terrain, pass under power lines near 4.1 miles and at 6.0 miles come to Road 222. Turn right and follow it up for about 0.6 mile to Nesmith Point.

Ferns on cliff wall of lower Nesmith Point Trail.

Elowah Falls

12

HIKE
DISTANCE: 2.0 miles round trip to Upper Elowah Falls; 1.6 miles round trip to Lower Elowah Falls
ELEVATION GAIN: 450 feet to Upper Elowah Falls round trip, 300 feet to Lower Elowah Falls round trip
HIGH POINT: 500 feet
ALLOW: 1 hour to Upper Elowah Falls round trip; 45 minutes to Lower Elowah Falls round trip
USUALLY OPEN: February through December

All routes in the Gorge are scenic, but the short, two-pronged trail to Upper and Lower Elowah Falls manages to cram in a most impressive amount of beauty and variety. The lower cascade is one voluminous flow and the upper one descends over a broad wall in many streamers. The two forks are also markedly different with the one to the lower falls following the floor of a lush, narrow canyon and the route to the upper traversing high on the sheer face of a 300-foot rock wall that affords a view of Mt. Adams.

VARIATIONS: The route past Lower Elowah Falls is concurrently the alignment of Gorge Trail No. 400 (No. 4) so the hike can be extended to the east. To understand why you can't follow Trail No. 400 to the west, take the Nesmith Point Trail (No. 11) at the start of the hike for 0.8 mile to *Elowah Falls.*

what was the junction of Trail No. 400 before the winter of '96-'97.

Approaching from the west, take I-84 to the Ainsworth Park Exit 35, at the end of the exit turn left, following the signs to Dodson and Warrendale, and in 150 feet turn right onto a frontage road. Travel east for 2.3 miles to the large parking area for Yeon State Park just before the road merges with the eastbound lanes of I-84. Coming from the east, take I-84 to the Dodson-Warrendale Exit 37. After going under the freeway turn left and proceed 0.4 mile to the parking area.

Follow the trail up from the west side of the parking lot, switchback and after 70 feet stay straight at the junction of the Nesmith Point Trail and Trail No. 400. Walk through a little cathedral of deciduous trees and then climb to the junction at 0.3 mile of the spur to the upper

falls. To visit it, turn right, traverse and then make several short switchbacks to the canyon wall. Travel along the sheer face, enter woods, have views of the falls, and come to the end of the tread at stream level.

Upper Elowah Falls.

To reach Lower Elowah Falls, contour to the east from the junction at 0.3 mile, descend into the canyon in six short switchbacks and walk upstream to the base of the falls.

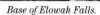

Base of Elowah Falls.

Munra Point

HIKE

13

DISTANCE: 5 miles round trip
ELEVATION GAIN: 2,050 feet round trip
HIGH POINT: 1,850 feet
ALLOW: 4 hours round trip
USUALLY OPEN: March through December

Munra Point is the distinctive little nubbin on the open ridge that forms the west wall of lower Tanner Creek canyon. Access to the use path, which pretty much makes a beeline to the summit area, is along a section of level Gorge Trail No. 400 (No. 4), so hikers have a warmup before tackling probably the steepest route in the Gorge. Because of this extreme grade, you should save this hike for a dry day after a period of no rain. Note that this is not an official trail, so don't attempt it if you know you feel comfortable only on signed, properly graded, and maintained routes.

VARIATION: You also can approach from the west along Gorge Trail No. 400 from Yeon State Park. This direction adds to 0.6 mile round trip.

Take I-84 to the Bonneville Dam Exit 40. From the T-junction at the south side of the interchange turn right and curve down to a parking area.

Walk back to the bridge over Tanner Creek, part of the original highway, after about 200 yards look for a trail heading up to the left and take it. The paved road that continues west is described in No. 15. Near the 1.0-mile point begin descending and after about 0.2-mile of downhill be

Tiger lily.

Hikers near the summit of Munra Point.

Munra Point from the north with Table Mountain and Greenleaf Peak in background.

watching for an obvious path on your left. It's not a big problem if you miss this junction because Trail No. 400 comes to the bridge over Moffett Creek in 0.1 mile.

Initially, climb at a reasonable angle but soon come to a steep section with a dirt surface, one of the most bothersome portions of the trip, going up and on the way back down. Continue climbing, but on a better tread. Be careful where you put your hands as poison oak thrives along portions of the route. Farther on you'll clamber up two steep little rocky outcroppings. Note landmarks around the top one because you can circumvent it on the left (south) on the return. Another outcropping farther on is little problem to come down.

At 1.9 miles traverse to the left, switchback once and come to the open face below the summit. Unfortunately, the tread of the path that contoured to the south and then climbed to the ridge crest has deteriorated to the degree that it's somewhat dangerous to follow. So, most hikers will opt to stop here at the face.

Wahclella Falls

HIKE

14

DISTANCE: 1.8 miles round trip
ELEVATION GAIN: 440 feet round trip
HIGH POINT: 380 feet
ALLOW: 1 hour round trip
USUALLY OPEN: February through December

Falls near the beginning of the trail.

*I*nfrequently is any place as enchanting as the wooded glen near the base of Wahclella Falls reached with so little effort. You will probably want to spend extra time here savoring the ambiance of the tall cedars, the pool, and the mist-producing cascade.

VARIATIONS: Although there are no side trips possible from the main route, sections of the Gorge Trail No. 400 (No. 4) and paved No. 15 both head west and east from the Wahclella Falls trailhead. Since you're in the neighborhood, you also could visit Bonneville Dam and the fish hatchery complex.

Take I-84 to the Bonneville Dam Exit 40. From the south side of the complex at a T-junction turn right and follow the unpaved road as it curves down to a parking area.

Walk south from the parking area along the road that parallels the east side of Tanner Creek. If you look up to the left you may be able to spot remains of the old flume that once carried water to the Bonneville fish hatchery. Pass the current intake system, begin walking on a trail and travel past the base of a high, thin waterfall on a long bridge.

Climb a stairway of broad steps and a bit farther come to a trail heading down slope that was, until the bridge that spanned Tanner Creek was torn off its footings, the lower end of a little loop. The bridge is scheduled to be replaced in 2001. However, because the

distances are so short, until then you can easily follow the western half of the loop to the other end of the ill-fated structure.

So, stay left and continue traversing the east wall of the narrow canyon. You will be able to see across and down to the other half of the loop as it crosses a slide that occurred in 1973. It dammed the creek and disrupted the water flow to the fish hatchery, although not long enough to do any damage. Descend a bit to the level area near the base of the falls.

To make the recommended side trip along the former (and future) route of the loop, continue down from the little area where you viewed the falls, cross a bridge, and traverse the rock slide.

Wahclella Falls.

Historic Columbia River Highway State Trail

15

BIKE/HIKE
DISTANCE: 7.8 miles round trip from Tanner Creek to Cascade Locks; 2.8 miles round trip west from Tanner Creek to Moffett Creek (No access from the west to Moffett Creek)
ELEVATION GAIN: 300 feet round trip to Cascade Locks; 200 feet round trip to Moffett Creek
HIGH POINT: 350 feet
ALLOW: 1 3/4 hours by bike and 4 hours on foot round trip to Cascade Locks; 1/2 hour by bike and 1 1/2 hours on foot round trip to Moffet Creek
USUALLY OPEN: February through mid-December

Fortunately, two sections of the original Columbia River Highway have been resurrected as pedestrian/bike paths. One goes between Hood River and Mosier (No. 30). The second one is open from Tanner Creek to Cascade Locks and by the fall of 2000 the route will be completed to the west as far as the bridge at Moffett Creek. Ultimately, the trail will continue west to Warrendale, but that is many years away. In addition to the scenic features, interesting, informative signs dot the way.

You have three access points:

TANNER CREEK: Take I-84 to the Bonneville Dam Exit 40 and go to the T-junction on the south side of the interchange. Either turn right and curve down to the trailhead parking for the Wahclella Falls Trail (No. 14) or turn left, head up the gravel road 0.2 mile to a T-junction, turn left, and descend to a large parking area.

EAGLE CREEK: Approaching from the west, take I-84 to the Eagle Creek Recreation Area Exit 41, turn right and park in the large area in front of the stone restroom building. To return west bound, head east on I-84 to the Cascade Locks Exit 44. Approaching from the east, take I-84 to the Bonneville Dam Exit 40 and travel east to the Eagle Creek exit.

CASCADE LOCKS: Take the Cascade Locks Exit 44 from I-84 to the parking area under the Bridge of the Gods at the far west end of the town. Note that the correct route is the paved, signed path adjacent to the west bound entrance road to the freeway.

Bridge of the Gods.

Mushrooms.

To investigate the section west from Tanner Creek to Moffett Creek, cross one of the original highway bridges, after 200 yards pass a section of Gorge Trail No. 400 (No. 4) and go under the freeway. Climb in a set of switchbacks and then travel parallel to, and also sometimes below, I-84 until the Moffett Creek Bridge.

The section from Tanner Creek east to Eagle Creek is 1.5 miles one way. Take the paved path that is between the gravel road to the easterly parking area and the entrance road to east bound I-84. Pass the main parking area and have an especially fun section where you travel past viewpoints above Tooth Rock Tunnel. Walk down the stairway to the exit road from I-84 and head east along the shoulder of the exit from I-84. Be reminded that briefly you are on a road where drivers will not be expecting you. From the T-junction at the end of the exit resume traveling on the paved path.

The section from Eagle Creek to Cascade Locks is 2.4 miles. Travel parallel to I-84 and then curve into an open area. The remainder of the trail is the best of an always enjoyable route. Enter woods, pass the bottom end of Ruckel Creek Trail (No. 18), 0.8 mile farther pass another section of Trail No. 400. Take a tunnel under the freeway and travel through woods to Cascade Locks.

Sunset with cottonwood trees.

Tanner Butte

Tanner Butte is the immense, treeless hulk of rock looming above the west side of the Eagle Creek drainage. The view from the summit is exceptionally far-ranging, extending from Mt. Jefferson north to Mt. Rainier and from Mt. Adams east to, on a really clear day, Saddle Mountain in the Oregon Coast Range. If you make the trip in late August, allow extra time for harvesting some of the huckleberries that line the upper section of the trail.

VARIATIONS: At 3.8 miles, a 0.3-mile spur takes you the 250 feet down to Dublin Lake. Midway along the return you can take the steep Tanner Cutoff Trail No. 448 and then a rustic, closed road back to your starting point, which involves no extra mileage. This lower loop alone makes a good hike.

Take I-84 to the Bonneville Dam Exit 40. From the T-junction on the south side of the interchange turn left onto the gravel road and climb 0.2 mile to a T-junction. Turn right and follow the narrow and extremely rough road 2.1 miles to the signed Tanner Butte Trail on your left at the head of a little side canyon. If you're planning to take Trail 448 up, walk along the road for 3.1 miles to the trailhead on your left. Meander for 0.6 mile to a junction and turn left onto the Tanner Cutoff Trail. The tread that continues straight here is noted in No. 11.

The initial 0.6 mile of the Tanner Butte Trail is over varied terrain and then the route begins switchbacking up at a steady, moderate grade. At 2.3

	HIKE
16	**DISTANCE:** 16 miles round trip
	ELEVATION GAIN: 3,800 feet round trip
	HIGH POINT: 4,500 feet
	ALLOW: 9 hours round trip
	USUALLY OPEN: June through November

Hiker in mist on lower part of trail.

continuing farther down along the path definitely is not recommended because of the severe erosion of several sections of the tread. Continue up from the junction on the main trail, at 3.7 miles come to the upper end of Trail 448 on your right and stay straight. By this point, you've done most of the climbing, except for the final section to the top. One-tenth mile farther pass the spur to Dublin Lake on your left.

Tanner Butte and Mt. Hood from Tanner Ridge.

Lower trail in fog.

miles, 0.1 mile beyond a small side stream, come to a possibly unsigned junction on your left. This 0.2 mile spur to wooded Wauna Point is an easy side trip, but

Walk on an old road bed and come to more open terrain where you'll have a view ahead to Tanner Butte. The easy cross-country route to the smaller summit to the east before the main one is a good stopping place if you want to shorten the hike. Cross a long, open saddle and about 0.4 mile beyond it be watching for a sign on your left identifying the Scramble Trail to the summit. As you near the summit the tread ends, so note landmarks that will help you locate the path for the return.

Eagle Creek Trail to Wahtum Lake

17

HIKE/BACKPACK
DISTANCE: 26.6 miles round trip
ELEVATION GAIN: 3,750 feet round trip
HIGH POINT: 3,750 feet
ALLOW: 12 hours round trip
USUALLY OPEN: June through November

For entirely good reasons, the lower portion of the trail through impressive Eagle Creek canyon is one of the most popular routes in the Gorge. Among many other visual delights, the tread traverses high along sheer rock walls and passes Metlako Falls, the Punch Bowl, and several other cascades before coming at 6.0 miles to unique Tunnel Falls, which makes an excellent destination. The grade to this point has been gentle, with 1,300 feet of elevation gain. Several good campsites are along the trail and at Wahtum Lake.

VARIATIONS: A demandingly fun loop can be made by taking Eagle-Benson Way at 5.0 miles up to Camp Smokey on the Pacific Crest Trail (No. 19) and following it north to connectors to the Ruckel Creek Trail (No. 18). This would be 15.3 miles

Punch Bowl Falls.

round trip with 4,200 feet of uphill. Backpackers who go to Wahtum Lake could, by establishing a short car shuttle or taking Trail 400 (No. 4), return on the PCT or the Herman Creek Trail (No. 20).

From the west take I-84 to the Eagle Creek Recreation Area Exit 41, turn right and parallel Eagle Creek for 0.7 mile to the road's end. To head westbound after the hike drive east to the Cascade Locks Exit 44. If you're approaching from the east go on I-84 to the Bonneville Dam Exit 40 and then head east.

Around 0.7 mile begin traveling along those sheer rock walls. Reenter less precipitous terrain, pass a path down to a view of Metlako Falls, cross Sorensen Creek, and at 1.8 miles come to the short spur down to creek level and a view upstream to Punch Bowl Falls, which you'll look down on a bit farther along the main trail. Cross four bridges, with the last two over Eagle Creek, at 5.0 miles come to the lower end of Eagle-Benson Trail and one mile farther go through the man-made cavern behind Tunnel Falls. A good food stop is on the rocky bank between the trail and Eagle Creek a short distance beyond the tunnel.

The main trail continues paralleling Eagle Creek for 1.6 miles to the junction of the infrequently taken Eagle-Tanner Trail, switchbacks left and begins a persistent climb. At 9.3 miles come to Inspiration Point with its fine views over lower Eagle Creek canyon. One-half mile farther stay straight (left) at the junction of a trail down from Indian Springs (see No. 26) and continue uphill the final 3.4 miles to the west end of Wahtum Lake. The trail on your left here crosses the outlet creek and connects with the PCT at Chinidere Mountain (No. 27). Walk above the shoreline and stay straight where the PCT comes down on the right. Above a camp area stay straight again where the continuation of the PCT heads left at a shallow angle. At the next fork you can take either one and climb to the rim above the lake. In addition to trails Nos. 26 and 27, Nos. 28 and 29 also begin from the end of the road above Wahtum Lake.

Log spanning upper Eagle Creek at Loowit Falls.

Metlako Falls.

Ruckel Ridge-Ruckel Creek Loop

18

HIKE
DISTANCE: 8.4 miles round trip
ELEVATION GAIN: 4,000 feet round trip
HIGH POINT: 3,700 feet
ALLOW: 5 1/2 hours round trip
USUALLY OPEN: early May through November

If you are an *experienced* hiker and in good condition, following the use path up the crest of Ruckel Ridge to the edge of the Benson Plateau is about the most fun 4,000 feet of steep uphill you'll ever have. Hikers who prefer official routes can take the sometimes moderately steep Ruckel Creek Trail, one of the most scenic in the Gorge, particularly in late April when the flowers in the hanging meadows are at their peaks.

Ruckel Ridge seems to be a magnet for people who grossly overestimate their hiking skills. If you are not accustomed to following use paths and have any problems with exposure, do not try this route. Qualified hikers making the trip for the first time should take Ruckel Ridge up.

VARIATIONS: By establishing a short car shuttle, hikers taking either route up could return on the Pacific Crest Trail (No. 19).

Coming from the west, take I-84 to the Eagle Creek Recreation Area Exit 41, turn right and park in front of the stone restroom building. To return west bound, drive east on I-84 to the Cascade Locks Exit 44. If you're approaching from the east, you first will have to take I-84 to the Bonneville Dam Exit 40.

View of Bonneville Dam from the Ruckel Creek Trail.

Walk east up the road for 75 yards to a sign on your left identifying the Gorge Trail No. 400 (No. 4). Climb and then walk along the edge of the campground to a fork. If you are intending to take the Ruckel Creek Trail up, stay left, descend and turn right onto a section of the original Columbia River Highway, which is now a pedestrian/bike path (No. 15). After 0.4 mile at the east side of the Ruckel Creek Bridge turn right onto the Ruckel Creek Trail.

To reach Ruckel Ridge, turn right at the fork, continue past more camp areas and begin climbing from site No. 5. After going under the power lines and reentering woods stay right, descend slightly and come to a large talus slope. Traverse across it for a few hundred feet and then be watching for a path that goes up to the left over the rocks. Aim for the little crest below the end of the cliff and follow it

up to the bottom of the sheer face. Turn left, follow along the base of the wall and then begin climbing very steeply on a well-defined use path. At 2.5 miles you can circumvent a very exposed catwalk by traversing below the crest on the west side. About 0.3 mile farther drop to a saddle and then begin the final mile of steep uphill to the junction with the Ruckel Creek Trail a short distance beyond the easy ford of Ruckel Creek.

If you intend to take the PCT back, turn right and be watching for the signed Benson Way on your left a short distance before Hunters Camp at Ruckel Creek. Benson Way meets the PCT in about 1.4 miles.

To head back along the Ruckel Creek Trail, turn left at the junction with the Ruckel Ridge route and soon begin winding downhill. Traverse the hanging meadows and then resume descending, passing an exposed viewpoint high above the Columbia River.

Hikers on Ruckel Ridge.

Spire above the Ruckel Creek Trail.

Pacific Crest Trail to Wahtum Lake

19

HIKE/BACKPACK
DISTANCE: 26 miles round trip
ELEVATION GAIN: 5,600 feet round trip
HIGH POINT: 4,300 feet
ALLOW: 13 to 14 hours round trip
USUALLY OPEN: June through November

Mounts Rainier and Adams and the valley holding the West Fork of Herman Creek from near Camp Smokey.

After dispatching most of the uphill in the initial 5.0 miles—at a comfortable grade and on a good surface because it is the Pacific Crest Trail, after all—this route covers the length of the Benson Plateau and then travels through a variety of terrain to Wahtum Lake (Nos. 17, 20, 26, 27, 28 and 29).

VARIATIONS: Two loop options for day hikers are to follow the Benson Way Trail from the north edge of the Benson Plateau to the Ruckel Creek Trail (No. 18) or continue to Camp Smokey below the south end of the Benson Plateau and take the Eagle-Benson Trail down to the Eagle Creek Trail (No. 17). Backpackers can return from Wahtum Lake on the Eagle Creek Trail or the Herman Creek Trail (No. 20). Note that all the loops but the last one would

Calypso orchid along the lower trail.

necessitate a short car shuttle, unless you choose to hike the extra 6.8 miles along Gorge Trail No. 400 (No. 4), which connects the lower trailheads.

Approaching from the west, take I-84 to the Cascade Locks Exit 44. Drive east through the town about 0.9 mile to a fork. Take either one to Forest Lane on the south side of I-84. Turn left on Forest Lane and head east for 0.4 mile if you took the left fork or 1.8 mile, passing the Oxbow Fish Hatchery, for the right one to the road up to Herman Creek Campground. If you're coming from the east, take I-84 to the Forest Lane-Herman Creek Road Exit 47. Go under the freeway, turn right and head west 0.5 mile. Drive up the road to trailhead parking at the far west side of the Campground area.

From the west side of the parking area, climb for a few tenths mile, cross a powerline access road and head up a short spur that soon narrows into a trail. Stay right at the

Section of the Pacific Crest Trail through the burn just south of the Benson Plateau with beargrass blooms in foreground.

junction of the route to the Gorton Creek, Herman Creek and Nick Eaton (No. 21) trails and descend to the bridge over Herman Creek. Climb a bit to the junction of the PCT, which began its Oregon section at Cascade Locks, turn left and begin the sustained climbing. Pass an overlook at 5.0 miles, then Teakettle Spring and less than one mile farther come to the edge of the Benson Plateau.

Unless you're making one of the loops, stay left on the PCT at the four connectors to the Ruckel Creek Trail and at 11.5 miles the junction of Eagle-Benson Way at Camp Smokey. Note that water, the first since Teakettle Spring unless you make side trips to Benson or Hunters Camp, is available a short distance down Eagle Benson Way. Beyond the south end of the Plateau cross a rocky slope and enter a small area that was burned in 1972. Traverse up in woods and 100 feet beyond the second switchback look for a spur on your left to an excellent overlook.

Continue traversing up and 175 feet beyond the 0.3 mile spur up to Chinidere Mountain come to the possibly unsigned trail down to the outlet end of Wahtum Lake. Stay straight, 0.4 mile farther be watching for the PCT heading off to the right at a shallow angle and follow it the final 1.4 miles to Wahtum Lake.

Herman Creek Trail

Camp Creek Falls.

20

HIKE/BACKPACK
DISTANCE: 24.4 miles round trip to Wahtum Lake
ELEVATION GAIN: 4,450 feet round trip
HIGH POINT: 4,400 feet (on the Anthill Trail)
ALLOW: 12 hours round trip
USUALLY OPEN: June through November

Continue on the level along the road, after about 300 yards pass the lower end of the Nick Eaton Trail and in another few hundred yards begin traveling on a trail.

You'll pass the lower ends of two trails that climb to the crest of Nick Eaton Ridge, Casey Creek Trail at 4.0 miles and at 7.3 miles the Herman Creek Cutoff Trail (refer to Nos. 22 and 29), which also connects with the Nick Eaton Trail. At 9.2 miles pass the 0.4-mile spur to Mud Lake. Climb for 0.5 mile to a junction of your right. You can reach Wahtum Lake this way (see No. 28), but the most straightforward route, if you're not familiar with the maze of trails in this area, is to stay left and continue up for 0.4 mile to a road. Cross it to the Anthill Trail, climb gently and then traverse to the end of the road above Wahtum Lake. In addition to Nos. 17 and 19, refer to Nos. 26, 27, 28 and 29 for more information on the trails in the Wahtum Lake area.

Decaying stump and devils club.

Most day hikers won't want to follow the Herman Creek all the way to Wahtum Lake and, fortuitously, they have an excellent stopping place at the 4.0-mile point with only 1,400 feet of uphill. In the relatively short distance you walk to reach this spot you have traveled through a variety of woods and terrain and past the bases of several fine, high waterfalls.

VARIATIONS: For a loop of 8.0 miles with 2,700 feet of climbing you could take the Casey Creek Trail up from the 4.0-mile point and return along the Nick Eaton Ridge or Gorton Creek trails (No. 21). With a short car shuttle, you could hike to the east or west along sections of Trail No. 400 (No. 4). Backpackers could return on the PCT (No. 19) or, by establishing a shuttle, on the Eagle Creek Trail (No. 17). Several more campsites are along the Herman Creek Trail beyond the 4.0-mile point.

Approaching from the west, take I-84 to Cascade Locks Exit 44. Drive east through the town about 0.9 mile to a fork. You can take either one as both take you to Forest Lane on the south side of I-84. Turn left onto Forest Lane and head east for 0.4 mile if you took the left branch or 1.8 miles, passing the Oxbow Fish Hatchery, for the right one to the road up to Herman Creek Campground at the Columbia Gorge Work Center. If you're coming from the east, take I-84 to the Forest Lane-Herman Creek Road Exit 47. Go under the freeway, turn right and head west for 0.5 mile. Drive up the paved road to trailhead parking at the west end of the camp area.

After winding up for a few tenths mile cross a powerline access road and head up a short spur that soon narrows to a trail. Turn left at the junction of the Herman Bridge Trail/Trail No. 400 that connects with the PCT and in a couple hundred yards come to a flat, open area at a sharp curve of an old road. Climb along the bed, eventually level off and at a clearing on your left at 1.4 miles pass the start of both the Gorton Creek Trail and the most easterly segment of Trail No. 400.

Hikers on trail in early winter.

Nick Eaton Ridge Indian Point Loop

Summit of Indian Point.

HIKE

21

DISTANCE: 9.0 miles round trip
ELEVATION GAIN: 3,450 feet round trip (including side trip to Indian Point)
HIGH POINT: 3,100 feet
ALLOW: 6 hours round trip
USUALLY OPEN: May through November

After winding up for a few tenths mile cross a powerline access road and head up a short spur that soon narrows to a trail. Turn left at the junction of the Herman Bridge Trail/Trail No. 400 (No. 4) that connects with the PCT (No. 19) and in a couple hundred yards come to a flat, open area. Walk up along the old road, eventually level off and at 1.4 miles pass a level area on the left and the lower end of the Gorton Creek Trail and the most easterly section of Trail No. 400. Continue along the road for about 300 yards and turn left onto the Nick Eaton Trail.

Meander up through a variety of woods and then open slopes to the junction at 3.4 miles of the 0.5-mile Ridge Cutoff Trail to the Gorton Creek Trail. Stay right and in several yards come to an open area with a view of Mt. Hood that is a good spot for a snack stop and 0.5 mile farther, after a short downhill stretch, come to the junction of the Deadwood Trail. Turn left and descend gently for 0.6 mile to the Gorton Creek Trail.

Nick Eaton Ridge forms the east wall of the lower Herman Creek drainage and its swaths of open slopes support noteworthy wildflower displays around mid-May. The loop described here follows an infrequently traveled connector to the Gorton Creek Trail from which the hike makes a short side trip to the base of Indian Point, a prominent rock outcropping on the wall of the Gorge.

VARIATIONS: You can shorten the loop to 7.1 miles and 3,300 feet of uphill by taking the Ridge Cutoff Trail to the Gorton Creek Trail. Or you can make a 10.6-mile loop with an additional 1,060 feet of elevation gain by continuing up to the crest of Nick Eaton Ridge and then returning along the Gorton Creek Trail. Other longer options are possible by taking routes that connect the Herman Creek Trail (No. 20) to Nick Eaton Ridge or by continuing to Green Point Mountain, the high point on the crest (refer to No. 22).

Approaching from the west, take I-84 to the Cascade Locks Exit 44. Drive east through the town about 0.9 mile to a fork. Take either branch to Forest Lane on the south side of I-84. Turn left on Forest Lane and head east for 0.4 mile if you took the left branch or for the right one 1.8 miles, passing the Oxbow Fish Hatchery, to the road up to Herman Creek Campground at the Columbia Gorge Work Center. If you're coming from the east, take I-84 to the Forest Lane-Herman Creek Road Exit 47. Go under the freeway, turn right and head west 0.5 mile. Drive up the paved road to trailhead parking at the west end of the camp area.

Wind and Dog mountains from Indian Point.

Turn left and after about 0.8 mile be watching for the obvious, but unsigned, steep spur down to the base of Indian Point. This is about 100 feet before you come to the junction of the north end of the Ridge Cutoff Trail. Do not climb on the pinnacle. The Gorton Creek Trail descends at a moderate grade and periodically offers good views to the north, despite its woodsy nature.

Ice-covered tree at Indian Point.

North Lake

North Lake.

HIKE

22

DISTANCE: 13.2 miles round trip
ELEVATION GAIN: 4,200 feet round trip
HIGH POINT: 4,000 feet
ALLOW: 8 hours round trip
USUALLY OPEN: late May through November

Following the Wyeth Trail to North Lake is a satisfyingly hard hike that, as an added bonus—and for no good reason—is not a heavily used route. People who do not consider climbing 4,200 feet a good thing can have a fine ending point at the last of the open slopes near 3.0 miles.

Trillium.

VARIATIONS: Hikers can continue another 1.1 miles beyond North Lake to Rainy Lake (refer to No. 29) or loop back to the Wyeth Trail along the Green Point Ridge Trail, which would add 2.6 miles and 650 feet of uphill. Trails connect east to Mt. Defiance (No. 24) and west over Green Point Mountain to the Gorton Creek and Nick Eaton Trails (refer to No. 21) and backpackers, by establishing a car shuttle, could take either of them back.

Drive on I-84 to the Wyeth Exit 51 and turn right if you're coming from the west or left if you're approaching from the east and come to a T-junction. Turn right and after about 0.2 mile turn left into Wyeth Campground. Drive, or walk if the road is closed, to the south, staying right where loops head off to the left, about 0.2 mile to the parking area at the end of the road. After the hike you are encouraged to drive west on the scenic road from the campground entrance. It connects with I-84 at Forest Lane for eastbound drivers and people heading west can continue to Cascade Locks.

Walk south on an old road for several hundred yards to the junction on your right of the eastern terminus of Gorge Trail No. 400 (No. 4). Turn left onto the Wyeth Trail and traverse up along the face of the slope. If the campground is closed, the unsigned path down on your left could be taken as a shortcut on the return. Walk along a powerline cut and then enter an exceptionally attractive woods of large vine maples

Woods along lower portion of the Wyeth Trail.

and widely spaced conifers. Along the lower middle portion a superb new alignment has replaced the very, very steep original grade. In addition to making for a considerably more comfortable climb, the new route was placed to take advantage of attractive open slopes that also afford good views.

Enter the Wilderness and continue up to the junction of the lower end of the Green Point Ridge Trail at 4.2 miles. Stay left on the Wyeth Trail, soon begin losing some of that hard-won elevation and have views of Mt. Defiance. Pass through an area that will be a bit swampy early in the season and resume climbing to the signed junction of the 30-yard spur to North Lake.

To make any of the side trips, from the junction just below North Lake continue south for 75 yards to a fork. To reach Mt. Defiance turn left and for the other options, turn right. To reach the upper end of the Green Point Ridge Trail, stay right at the junction of the trail to Rainy Lake and 0.5 mile farther turn right onto the Green Point Ridge Trail at the junction with the Gorton Creek Trail.

Cabin Creek Loop

HIKE

23

DISTANCE: 1.9 miles round trip
ELEVATION GAIN: 1,000 feet round trip
HIGH POINT: 700 Feet
ALLOW: 1 1/2 hours round trip
USUALLY OPEN: February through December

This fun and scenically varied little loop combines the lowest portions of the Starvation Ridge and Mt. Defiance Trails (No. 24). The circuit passes two impressive waterfalls, but the most noteworthy terrain is the expanse of open slopes that affords views over the Columbia River and across to the Washington side. Although always charming, the hike is at its very best around mid-April when those open slopes are colorful with wildflowers. Be prepared for three stream fords, which are not at all difficult but will most likely get your boots and socks wet.

VARIATIONS: You are encouraged to wind up the Starvation Ridge Trail for an additional 0.4 mile and 500 feet to the last viewpoint before that route enters woods. Here is an excellent place to watch the river traffic below and try to spot hikers on Dog Mountain (No. 38). Before or after the hike you'll want to head east from the parking area beyond the closed restrooms to view Starvation Falls.

If you're approaching from the west, take I-84 to between the 55 and 56 mile posts to the former Starvation Creek Rest Area. After the

Shooting stars line the lower Starvation Ridge Trail.

Walk west from the parking lot to the big sign that identifies the Mt. Defiance Trail, parallel the freeway on the south side of a cement barricade and soon begin walking on a section of the original Columbia River Highway. A few hundred yards from the start come to the signed Starvation Cutoff Trail on your left. Although this description is counter-clockwise because that saves the gentler grade for the downhill return, you can reverse the direction.

Turn left and wind up for 0.5 mile to the junction with the Starvation Ridge Trail. The grade becomes considerably more gentle for the final 0.2 mile. For the recommended side trip, turn left at the junction and wind up in 14 switchbacks across the open slope and periodically in woods to the ridge crest. To continue the loop, follow the main trail down from the junction at 0.6 mile and ford Cabin Creek. Climb out of the little canyon to a crest and pass a short path to an overlook. Wind down open slopes, ford Warren Creek and continue traversing down along the powerline cut to the junction with the Mt. Defiance Trail. Turn right and descend to a second ford of Warren Creek below Hole-in-the-Wall Falls. Turn left immediately after the crossing, go through an ever-shrinking clearing and reenter woods. Meet the old highway bed and pass Cabin Creek Falls just before the junction of the Cutoff Trail.

Cabin Creek Falls in winter.

hike, drivers wanting to head westbound will need to drive east on I-84 for 0.8 mile to the Viento State Park Exit 56. If you're coming from the east, drive to the Wyeth Exit 51 and then head back to the east. The restrooms have been closed for some time and the State has not yet determined the eventual use for the area. However, you can maneuver around the barricades and park in the lot.

Starvation Falls.

Starvation Ridge—Mt. Defiance Loop

24

HIKE
DISTANCE: 13.5 miles round trip
ELEVATION GAIN: 5,300 feet round trip
HIGH POINT: 4,960 feet
ALLOW: 8 hours round trip
USUALLY OPEN: June through October

Mt. Defiance is the highest point in the Columbia River Gorge and the trek to it has always been a classic conditioning hike. Combining the Mt. Defiance Trail with the Starvation Ridge Trail provides twice the scenery for your effort. However, note the 0.8-mile section above Warren Lake that connects the two routes is along a sometimes faint use path.

VARIATION: If you want only to follow the Starvation Ridge Trail to its end at Warren Lake, you will have 12.0 miles round trip and 4,100 feet of elevation gain.

Approaching from the west, take I-84 to between the 54 and 55 mile posts to the closed Starvation Creek Rest Area. Coming from the east, drive to the Wyeth Exit 51 and then head back to the east. You can maneuver around the barricades and park in the lot. After the hike, people wanting to head westbound will need to go east on I-84 to the Viento State Park Exit 56.

Walk west from the parking lot to the big sign identifying the Mt. Defiance Trail and parallel the freeway on the south side of the cement barricade. After several hundred yards turn left onto the signed Starvation Cutoff Trail, because taking this route will save almost 1.5 miles and three stream crossings. If you are taking the Mt. Defiance Trail up, continue straight. Climb steeply for 0.5 mile to the junction with the Starvation Ridge Trail (No. 23) and turn left. Wind up impressive, steep grassy slopes and occasionally in groves of oaks and firs to an open crest.

Frost-covered leaves.

Warren Falls in winter.

Follow the ridge crest and soon enter woods, which have sufficient variety to keep you visually amused until around 4.5 miles where you come to the first evidence of past logging activity. At the junction of a route that goes to a road, turn right and descend for 0.4 mile to Warren Lake.

To continue the loop, head west from the junction 50 yards above the lake, walk around the north shore and then wind up in a generally westerly direction along a sometimes obscure tread to the Mt. Defiance Trail. If you meet it at just the right spot you'll climb for about 0.1 mile to where the main route turns right. The path on the left is a shortcut down from the summit. For now, take the official route along the open slopes because it offers views you'll not see from the summit. On the southwest side of the peak come to the junction of the trail that descends past the spur to Bear Lake, turn left and make the final short climb to the summit and its plethora of microwave installations.

To take the shortcut back, walk to the northeast corner of the most northerly building and look for the path. Cross the road twice, veering right the second time to pick up the path. As with the climb, the descent offers a variety of scenery. The only junction you'll meet is that of the Starvation Ridge Trail near the end. Stay left, continue down to the easy ford of Warren Creek, veer left, go through a little clearing and then head east to the starting point.

Wygant Peak

Oregon white oaks along the lower Wygant Trail.

Looking west from a viewpoint along the lower Wygant Trail.

25	HIKE
	DISTANCE: 8.1 miles round trip
	ELEVATION GAIN: 2,200 feet round trip
	HIGH POINT: 2,214 feet
	ALLOW: 4 hours round trip
	USUALLY OPEN: March through November

Although there may be no panoramas from Wygant Peak's wooded summit, the trail that climbs to it delightfully meanders through an astounding variety of attractive terrain and periodically affords fine views to the north, including Wind, Dog (No. 38) and Augsperger mountains, beyond to Mt. Adams and directly down onto the Columbia River.

VARIATIONS: You have the opportunity to make a fun side loop along the middle portion of the descent. Note this does involve a ford that is not difficult, but probably will get your feet wet. From the summit you could continue along the trail for 0.2 mile, losing 200 feet, to a meadow with a view of Mt. Defiance (No. 24). And before or after the hike you can explore the Mitchell Point Overlook at the parking area.

From the west, drive on I-84 to the Mitchell Point Overlook Exit 58. At the end of the exit turn right and then left and come to a parking area. The imposing rock mass overhead is Mitchell Point, the site of a former tunnel on the original Columbia River Highway. Unfortunately, it was destroyed for the construction of I-84. To return westbound, continue east on the freeway to Exit 62. Those approaching from the east first will have to go to the Viento State Park Exit 56.

Walk back to the junction where you turned left and continue west along a road. Where it curves sharply up to the left stay straight and in several yards begin traveling on a trail. Descend back to the old highway, follow it for about 0.3 mile to a side canyon and turn left. Soon cross to the west wall and begin climbing. Just before you come to the canyon holding Perham Creek note the Chetwoot Trail on your left, which is the route of the recommended return loop. Descend to the bridge across the stream and resume climbing, mostly through oak forests, and pass several viewpoints. At the first overlook the trail almost doubles back on itself as it reenters woods. The free-standing outcropping to the west on the Oregon side of the Gorge is Indian Point (No. 21). At 2.7 miles at the end of a second long traverse where the trail switchbacks to the right watch for the possibly unsigned upper end of the Chetwoot Trail, which continues to the east. For now, make the switchback and continue circuitously winding up in woods, which become ever more lushly coniferous, but not so verdant that you still don't have views to the north.

The tread of the return loop on the Chetwoot Trail is a bit more rustic than that of the Wygant Trail but that, and the opportunity to enjoy even more of the varied terrain, adds to the route's lure. Beyond the ford, where you come to the powerline cut head east about 150 feet and then head left back into the woods.

Indian Mountain

26

BIKE/HIKE
DISTANCE: 8.0 miles round trip by bike; 9.0 miles round trip hiking, mostly on the Pacific Crest Trail
ELEVATION GAIN: 1,626 foot by bike; 1,627 foot on the Pacific Crest Trail
HIGH POINT: 4,900 feet
ALLOW: 2.1/2 hours round trip by bike; 4 1/2 hours round trip hiking on the PCT
USUALLY OPEN: July through mid-October

Deciduous tree branch in snow.

All four trips in this guide that begin from the saddle above Wahtum Lake (Nos. 26 through 29) afford exceptionally far-ranging views, but the most extensive is from Indian Mountain. To the south beyond nearby Mt. Hood are Mt. Jefferson, Olallie Butte and the terrain comprising the Bull of the Woods area and to the east lies the Upper Hood River Valley. The view north extends over the Gorge from nearby Tanner Butte to Mt. Defiance and into Washington to mounts St. Helens, Rainier and Adams.

Mountain cyclists follow roads and hikers the Pacific Crest Trail to a broad, open crest and from there both share the final distance to the summit. Cyclists are reminded that bikes are not permitted on the PCT and are forewarned that the beginning portions of the shared route are very rough.

VARIATIONS: Mountain bikers can explore the side roads that head off from the main route or they also could combine the ride with the one along Waucoma Ridge (No. 29). Hikers have the option of a loop, which would add 2.8 miles and 1,150 feet of uphill, by taking the trail from Indian Springs down to the Eagle Creek Trail and then following it up to Wahtum Lake.

From Dee, in the Upper Hood River Valley, cross the bridge and turn left onto Lost Lake Road. Follow it for 5.0 miles to the signed road on the right to Wahtum Lake, 4.5 miles farther stay right and continue along paved, but narrow, Road 1310 the final 6.0 miles to the trailhead. You also can reach Lost Lake Road from Lolo Pass, but for most people it's easier to take Oregon 35 and secondary roads to Dee.

If you're doing the trip by bike, from the parking area head south up unpaved Road 660. Stay right in 0.5 mile and soon have a view down onto Scout Lake. After 0.6 mile stay right again, begin riding on a more rustic surface and in 1.3 miles stay left where a short spur goes to Indian Springs. Stay right after 0.4 mile, shortly come to a berm and ride almost 0.2 mile farther to the crest of the ridge. Turn left here and follow the faint, rocky road along the crest. Eventually, it

enters woods and becomes smoother. Where the road ends at a trail, which may have a few fallen trees over it, climb the final short distance to the summit.

If you're doing the trip as a hike, from the bulletin board on the north side of the parking area head down to Wahtum Lake. Stay straight at the junction of the trail that goes around the south shore and in a short distance turn left and begin climbing on the PCT. Where you come to Indian Springs at 3.1 miles look for the resumption of the PCT across the clearing. The connector down to the Eagle Creek Trail, which may not be signed, begins from the center of the clearing and soon passes the spring. Where you come to the crest of the ridge, turn left, leaving the PCT. Cross the road the cyclists took in and continue up the crest, following the same route as described for them.

Looking from Tanner Ridge across Opal and Eagle Creek drainages to Indian Mountain.

Chinidere Mountain

HIKE

27

DISTANCE: 3.8 miles round trip
ELEVATION GAIN: 1,145 feet round trip
HIGH POINT: 4,673 feet
ALLOW: 3 hours round trip
USUALLY OPEN: late June through mid-October

The view from Chinidere Mountain above Wahtum Lake is one of the best in the Gorge, extending from Mt. Jefferson past much of the Gorge and north to Mt. Rainier.

VARIATIONS: The basic hike is actually a loop that, when completed, has circled Wahtum Lake. One extension is to head north on the Pacific Crest Trail (No. 19) for an additional 1.5 miles to a viewpoint or continue another 1.1 miles to Camp Smokey on the southern edge of the Benson Plateau. A hard loop of 11.5 miles with 3,000 feet of uphill would be to take the connector from Camp Smokey down to the Eagle Creek Trail (No. 17) and follow it up to Wahtum Lake. For a much easier loop, you can combine the Chinidere Mountain and the southern part of the Tomlike Mountain (No. 28) hikes.

From Dee, in the Upper Hood River Valley, cross the bridge and turn left onto Lost Lake Road. Follow it for 5.0 miles to the signed road on the right to Wahtum Lake, 4.5 miles farther stay right on paved, but narrow, Road 1310 and take it the final 6.0 miles to the trailhead. You also can reach Lost Lake Road from Lolo Pass, but for most people it's easier to take Oregon 35 and then secondary roads to Dee.

From the bulletin board at the parking area take either trail down—the one to the right is smooth and gentler, the one to the left has steps. Beyond where they merge walk above the southern shore and come to a junction. If you make the loop described here, you'll be returning along the path to

Bracket fungus on tree stump.

the right. Stay left and then stay right where the Pacific Crest Trail heads up slope to Indian Springs (refer to No. 26). In a short distance come to the junction of the Eagle Creek Trail.

Turn right, descend briefly and cross the outlet of Wahtum Lake on a tangle of big logs. Pass some campsites and wind up, crossing a stream near the top, to a possibly unsigned junction. Turn left onto the PCT and after about 200 feet come to the 0.3-mile spur up to Chinidere Mountain. If you're making the hike when wildflowers are blooming, absolutely take the PCT north to the open slopes of Chinidere Mountain because they are smothered with a delightfully impressive variety of blossoms.

Wahtum Lake from the summit of Chinidere Mountain.

To complete the loop, return to the junction just south of the spur to Chinidere Mountain, stay straight and travel on the level for 0.4 mile to a trail angling gently off to the right. If you keep straight here you pass the connector to the Herman Creek Trail and, if you continued straight again, you would soon meet the abandoned road that goes to the parking area (No. 29). To complete the loop, turn right, initially walk on the level through an area that will be somewhat swampy early in the season and then begin gently descending. Where you come to the junction you passed on the hike in, turn left and retrace your route to the start.

Looking north from the summit of Chinidere Mountain to the Benson Plateau with Mt. St. Helens in background.

Mt. Hood from the summit of Chinidere Mountain.

Tomlike Mountain

Tomlike Mountain is the highest point on Woolly Horn Ridge, which separates the East and West Forks of Herman Creek. In addition to the far-ranging views, which extend from mounts St. Helens, Rainier and Adams to Mt. Hood, the hike involves a bit of easy cross-country travel, a fun opportunity not common in the Gorge.

VARIATIONS: Because of the network of interconnecting trails, you have the option of three return loops. The most straightforward is to take the trail along the north and east sides of Wahtum Lake. Another route back is along the trail that drops to the west (outlet) end of Wahtum Lake. If you follow the latter, you're encouraged also to make the short side climb to Chinidere Mountain (No. 27). A third option is to follow the old road that traverses between the lake and the Anthill Trail, which you'll be taking in.

From Dee, in the Upper Hood River Valley, cross the bridge and turn left onto Lost Lake Road. Follow it for 5.0 miles to the signed road on the right to Wahtum Lake, 4.5 miles farther stay right and continue along paved, but narrow, Road 1310 the final 6.0 miles to the trailhead. You also can reach Lost Lake Road from Lolo Pass, but for most people it's easier to take Oregon 35 and secondary roads to Dee.

Take the Anthill Trail, which begins behind the outhouses, for 1.9 miles to an old road, which extends from Wahtum Lake to just below Rainy Lake (No. 29). Cross it and begin descending on the Herman Creek Trail (No. 20). After 0.4 mile note the trail that heads left

HIKE

28

DISTANCE: 6.0 miles round trip
ELEVATION GAIN: 1,090 feet round trip
HIGH POINT: 4,555 feet
ALLOW: 4 hours round trip
USUALLY OPEN: July through mid-October

conifers. The remainder of the hike follows an obvious tread up to the summit.

Return to the junction below the road noted earlier, stay right and climb at a gentle grade to the crest, which is the divide between the Eagle Creek and Herman Creek drainages. Descend equally gently to a junction. To take the road back, turn left and where you come to the old bed turn right. For the other two options, stay right. The junction of the route that eventually traverses above the north and east shores angles back to the left after about 0.3 mile and the junction of the route to the outlet end is about 0.4 mile farther. It is obvious but may be unmarked (refer to No. 27 for details). For either of the trails to the lake, where you come to junctions on the south shore turn left. At an unsigned fork you can climb on steps or stay left and rise more gently to the start of the hike.

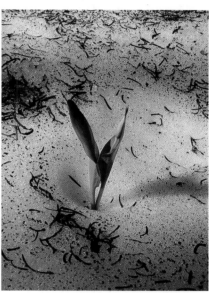

Avalanche lily in late spring near Wahtum Lake.

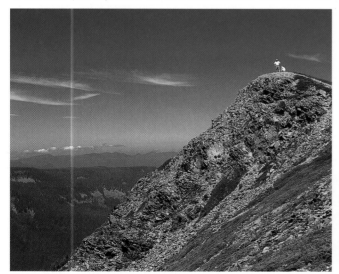

Hikers on the summit of Tomlike Mountain.

because you will be taking it for any of the return loops. Continue on the Herman Creek Trail another 100 feet and, where it turns right, keep straight (left) on an unmarked path. After another 100 feet stay right at a fork and soon begin skirting the rocky edge of the ridge. Descend to a broad saddle, resume climbing and where you come to a boulder swath veer left, traverse along the southwest face and then curve back to the crest. Continue up the crest a short distance and find the path that winds through a little grove of short, very dense

Mt. Adams from the summit of Tomlike Mountain.

Waucoma Ridge

29

BIKE
DISTANCE: 11.4 miles round trip
ELEVATION GAIN: 1,065 feet round trip
HIGH POINT: 4,480 feet
ALLOW: 3 hours round trip
USUALLY OPEN: Late June through October

Extending northeast from Wahtum Lake, Waucoma Ridge straddles the boundary between the Columbia River Gorge and the Hood River Valley. Sections of the abandoned road along this crest afford far-ranging views into—and beyond—both regions. At the east end, riders can leave their bikes and make the 0.3-mile walk to Rainy Lake in the Mark O. Hatfield Wilderness.

This trip certainly could be done as a hike, but it's particularly suited for mountain biking by riders of intermediate or better skills.

VARIATIONS: Bicyclists have few options because all the trails they pass on the west immediately enter the Wilderness, where bikes absolutely are prohibited. Cyclists who enjoy single track can take the Anthill Trail on the return. Another bike route (No. 26) shares the same starting point and the two could be combined for a full day's worth of riding.

Beargrass at sundown.

Hikers could explore a bit of the route by taking the Anthill Trail north, following the road along Waucoma Ridge for only several tenths mile to excellent viewpoints and then returning along one of the trails described in No. 28.

From Dee, in the Upper Hood River Valley, cross the bridge over the West Fork of the Hood River and turn left onto Lost Lake Road. Follow it for 5.0 miles to the signed road on the right to Wahtum Lake, 4.5 miles farther stay right and continue along paved, but narrow, Road 1310 the final 6.0 miles to the trailhead. You also can reach Lost Lake Road from Lolo Pass, but for most people it's easier to take Oregon 35 and secondary roads to Dee.

If you're biking, head northeast from the parking area along the unpaved road and after about 100 feet

come to a gate. As you traverse the often lumpy road you'll have occasional glimpses down to Wahtum Lake. For the entire ride, you'll find that just about the time you've become thoroughly irritated with the rough surface, it becomes considerably smoother. At 2.4 miles come to an open area where the Anthill Trail comes in on the right and the Herman Creek Trail (closed to bikes) heads down to the left. You'll have particularly good viewpoints at 2.7 and 3.1 miles that include sightings of mounts Hood and St. Helens and over the Herman Creek drainage.

Beyond 3.3 miles you'll begin riding on generally smoother surfaces. And, although the grade is mostly downhill, between 4.0 and 4.3 miles you'll have a level stretch in woods. Farther on the terrain is open again with views to the south. Have a last rough traverse and then bob through woods in little ups and downs to the turnaround at the trail to Rainy Lake.

Indian paintbrush.

Woolly Horn Ridge from north of Wahtum Lake.

Mosier Tunnel

30

BIKE/HIKE
DISTANCE: 10.2 miles round trip (A short car shuttle makes one way trips possible)
ELEVATION GAIN: 700 feet round trip
HIGH POINT: 500 feet
ALLOW: 2 1/2 hours round trip by bike; 7 hours round trip hiking
USUALLY OPEN: February through December

Among the most lamented features of the original Columbia River Highway that were destroyed or altered by the construction of I-84 was the Mosier Tunnel east of Hood River. Fortunately, this unique landmark had been filled-in, not obliterated and renovation of the tunnel was completed in the summer of 2000.

VARIATIONS: Hikers could establish a short car shuttle. Because of the minimal elevation gain, bicyclists might want to begin 1.2 miles and about 300 feet below the western end so they could have a bit more of a workout. Similarly, they can start in the town of Mosier and have an extra 0.6 mile and 200 feet of uphill from that end. Also, both road

Tug and barge below the Bingen Anticline in Washington from the viewpoint just east of the tunnel.

and mountain cyclists can make a loop by returning along I-84. Those with mountain bikes can explore the unpaved road that heads up from the eastern parking lot and, according to maps, eventually descends to Hood River.

Another paved pedestrian/bike route along a section of the original Columbia River Highway is No. 15 between Moffett Creek and Cascade Locks.

To reach the western end, take I-84 to Exit 64 and follow the signs to Oregon 35 and Government Camp. After about 0.4 mile come to a four-way stop and turn left. If you're a cyclist wanting that extra work park off to the right after the turn. Drive (or bike) 1.2 miles to the parking area, for which those with cars must pay $3.00.

To reach the eastern parking area, take I-84 to the Mosier Exit 69. As you leave the elevated exit and level off look for a signed road heading off to your left and turn onto it. If you're a bicyclist who wants that extra distance and

Juvenile raccoon.

climbing, where you level off don't turn but stay straight for 0.1 mile to a large parking area on the left across from a grocery store. Drive (or bike) under the ramp and begin climbing. About 0.6 mile from Mosier come to a road on your right to handicapped parking and the trailhead. If driving, stay left and continue the short distance to the main parking area, where the fee also is $3.00 and there are restrooms.

Both ends of the route are in woods, but the composition of each is remarkably different, considering the short distance that separates them. Beginning from the west the towns on the Washington side you'll see after a couple tenths mile are White Salmon and Bingen. Between 1.6 and 2.0 miles travel through an inner valley, at 3.9 miles come to the tunnel. The attractive wood wall and ceiling covering replicates the original design of the tunnel. On the other side pass an especially attractive overlook area and descend for 0.8 mile to the eastern trailhead.

Grass widows.

Wasco Butte

Small lake near the summit of Wasco Butte.

31
BIKE
DISTANCE: 19.5 miles round trip
ELEVATION GAIN: 2,300 feet round trip
HIGH POINT: 2,346 feet
ALLOW: 3 hours round trip
USUALLY OPEN: late February through November

From Mosier this mountain-bike ride follows paved roads past cherry orchards and then travels along unpaved routes that alternate between traversing woods and open slopes and provide far-ranging and considerably less common views, including ones of Mt. Hood. Most of the way back is along a different route, so you'll enjoy even more of the varied scenery. Because of those cherry trees, the ride is particularly attractive in May when they bloom and in early October when the leaves turn red.

VARIATION: Those interested in riding 14 more miles could begin and end at the west end of the Mosier Tunnel trip (No. 30).

Drive on I-84 to the Mosier Exit 69 and in about 0.4 mile come to a large area for parking on the left across from the Mosier Market and the base of Washington Street.

Bicycle up Washington Street and turn left onto Third Ave., which farther on is identified as State Road. At 0.7 mile stay left, immediately cross a bridge and turn right,

watching for the dangerous grate with an open grid, onto Carroll Road. In 0.1 mile stay right on Carroll Road at the junction of Dry Creek Road, which you'll be following on the return loop, and ride mostly very steeply uphill on Carroll Road for 1.8 miles past those orchards to a T-junction. Turn right and come to the end of the pavement.

At 3.5 miles stay left, following the signs to American Adventure, and 0.8 miles farther stay right at the entrance to it. Be sure to note the junction on your left at 5.8 miles of the Osburn Cutoff because it is the route you'll be taking after you explore Wasco Butte. Now, however, stay right and 0.6 mile farther stay left at a fork and climb rather steeply above a farm. Reenter an oak forest and at 7.6 miles in an open area turn left onto a possibly unsigned road just before the main route descends over the other side of the ridge.

In 0.4 mile stay right, 0.1 mile farther stay left and in another 0.1 mile come to the summit. Those other roads merit exploring,

Small ranch near Wasco Butte.

particularly the one 0.4 mile above the main road because it goes to a lake.

For the return loop, retrace your route to Osburn Cutoff, turn right, follow it down for 2.5 miles and turn left onto Dry Creek Road. After 2.9 miles stay straight (left) at the junction of Morgensen Road, continuing on Dry Creek Road, and begin traveling on pavement. Have 2.6 miles of fun, easy downhill to the junction with Carroll Road, which you took in, turn right and go the final 0.9 miles to the start.

Summit of Mt. Hood from the road to Wasco Butte.

Tom McCall Park

HIKE
32

DISTANCE: 1.6 miles round trip for lower trail; 3.0 miles round trip for upper trail
ELEVATION GAIN: 300 feet round trip for lower trail; 1,180 feet round trip for upper trail
HIGH POINT: 1,900 feet (summit of upper trail)
ALLOW: 3/4 hour for lower trail round trip; 2 hours for upper trail round trip
LOWER TRAIL USUALLY OPEN: Late February through December
UPPER TRAIL OPEN: from May through October

Small lake at Tom McCall Park.

Looking down onto a tug and barge on the Columbia River and the town of Lyle.

Old rock fence west of the Rowena Loops.

hanks to The Nature Conservancy, 231 acres on Rowena Crest, the high point above the Columbia River between Mosier and The Dalles, have been preserved for outdoor lovers. Two trails cover the area. The lower route, which even includes a lake, loops over mostly open terrain that is especially noted for its wildflower displays in early to mid-spring. The other trail climbs to a viewpoint high on the southern edge of the preserve.

The Nature Conservancy requests that you remember this is a nature preserve, not a park. To ensure it is undamaged in the present and for future visitors, some restrictions apply for the use of this area, but they hardly diminish your enjoyment. No dogs are permitted in the preserve. Stay on the established trails and note that the upper one is closed from November through April to lessen soil erosion. If you plan to visit with 10 or more people, phone The Nature Conservancy and inform them of this so they can provide a guide. And, as with all areas, never pick the flowers or any vegetation. And watch out for rattlesnakes, poison oak, ticks and steep cliffs.

The drive is almost as scenic as the destination. And you are encouraged to continue east after the hike and wind down the Rowena Loops, rejoining I-84 at the west end of The Dalles. Take I-84 to the Mosier Exit 69, drive east through the community on what becomes US 30 and pass a sign stating Rowena Crest Viewpoint 6 miles. The trailheads are at the crest adjacent to the entrance to the loop road that goes to a large viewing area, which you also will want to visit.

With its open slopes, the expansive setting of the lower route lends itself to leisurely ambling. Follow the trail down to a fork and then take either branch and make a loop around a lake. The high cliffs offer a dramatic contrast to the relatively gentle terrain above their rims. The upper trail begins across the road and with its relatively denser vegetation has a markedly different ambiance than the lower one.

Deschutes River

BIKE/HIKE
DISTANCE: 38.8 miles round trip
ELEVATION GAIN: 300 feet round trip
HIGH POINT: 400 feet
ALLOW: 5 to 6 hours round trip by bike
USUALLY OPEN: mid-February through December

33

For hikers and cyclists accustomed to the lush vegetation on the west slope of the Cascades, experiencing the openness and clarity of the terrain at the east end of the Gorge is an invigorating change. Following a former railroad grade that parallels the east side of the Deschutes River takes you through some of the prime landscape in this area. The best times to visit are spring and fall because summers are hot and winters are frigid. In spring, a bonus will be the sighting of many goslings on the bank and river. At any time, however, you will enjoy the grand scenery and the historical remains of railroad construction and ranching activity.

Of course, hikers and backpackers will savor this area also, but taking the road on a mountain bike enables the visitor to go a lot farther in the same amount of time. A few sections of the almost entirely level bed are rough, but even a bike without suspension can manage them using somewhat lower tire pressures.

VARIATIONS: Those who visit on foot have the option of a few short trails, both above and below the road. For mountain bikers this is a simple out and back route. Since the entire ride is scenic, any turnaround point makes for a satisfying outing.

Drive on I-84 to Exit 97 east of The Dalles and follow Oregon 206 as it parallels the freeway for 3.3 miles to the entrance to Deschutes State Park, just beyond where you cross the Deschutes River. Turn right and park in the area to the east. If you want to visit the restrooms and picnic area stay right. Pedal or walk along the unpaved road that heads south from the parking area. Watch out for snakes stretched out across the road. Where you are close enough, determine

Old railroad trestle along the lower Deschutes River.

which is the tail end and ride past on that side. Don't run over them—after all, they live here and you're just visiting. Initially, the grade is gently uphill, but the remainder of the route is level, except for one short descent and climb at 3.2 miles.

You will notice tracks along the opposite side of the river—and even, perhaps, see a freight—and ask yourself why there also would be a railroad on the east side. Two different companies were building lines and the competition to finish first involved the opposing crews lobbing dynamite and rattlesnakes across the river—and worse. Ultimately, Congress had to decide which side would be allowed to complete the project.

At 11.5 miles pass an old farmhouse and just beyond it some buildings adjacent to the road. This is a good turnaround point for cyclists wanting a moderately long ride, even though there are more remains of the former ranch farther on. Most riders will opt to go no farther than 19.4 miles because at this point the trestle is gone and crossing the canyon it spanned would require a ford.

Aerial of the mouth of the Deschutes River.

Beacon Rock

34

HIKE

DISTANCE: 1.6 miles round trip
ELEVATION GAIN: 600 feet round trip
HIGH POINT: 850 feet
ALLOW: 1 hour round trip
USUALLY OPEN: All year except during periods of extreme weather, at which times the gate at the lower end of the trail is locked.

As you corkscrew up Beacon Rock, the distinctive formation on the north side of the Columbia River west of Bonneville Dam, you can't help but marvel that one person, who at the time owned the rock, and a helper built the original trail between 1915 and 1918. For rock climbers, reaching the summit is a challenge, but hikers follow the excellent trail, which has been made safe with railings and catwalks when

Looking east down onto the Columbia River from the summit of Beacon Rock.

Hikers winding up the south side of Beacon Rock.

necessary. From the top the views up and down the Gorge are, not surprisingly, extensive and engrossing.

VARIATION: After the climb you could investigate a nature area on the west side of Beacon Rock. The first network of trails here fell into disrepair, but Park personnel intend to rebuild them as funds become available. However, one section to a small lake remains open and it is interesting to explore.

Drive on Washington 14 for 6.9 miles west of the Bridge of the Gods, which is accessible from I-84 at Cascade Locks, or 28.4 miles east of the I-205 Bridge to parking on the south side of the road just to the east of Beacon Rock. Additional space also is available just west of the rock at the clearing at the start of the nature trail.

Walk to the west side of Beacon Rock, originally named Castle Rock, and take the signed trail through woods. Veer left and begin zigzagging uphill. Early on you'll pass a gate that is closed when the trail is unsafe. After 40 switchbacks, traverse around to the east side and then have seven more turns before coming to the top. Hamilton Mountain (No. 36) is immediately to the northeast and Nesmith Point (No. 11) is the high point on the rim across the Columbia River. To explore the nature trail, go to the open area to the west of Beacon Rock and look for a path heading south from near the east side of the clearing. It is open for about 0.4 mile to a little lake. If you try to follow any of the overgrown treads, watch out for nettles.

Aerial view of the south side of Beacon Rock.

Dogwood blossoms.

Hardy Creek

35

BIKE
DISTANCE: 11.3 miles round trip
ELEVATION GAIN: 2,600 feet round trip
HIGH POINT: 2,300 feet
ALLOW: 3 hours round trip
USUALLY OPEN: March through November

Mountain bicyclists on the north end of Hamilton Ridge.

Cliffs on the south side of Hamilton Mountain.

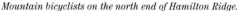
Deciduous tree felled by beaver.

Midway along this ride to the west of Hamilton Mountain you come to an impressive viewpoint on the broad open saddle at the north end of the peak's summit ridge. In addition to many other landmarks, from here you'll have an especially interesting view to the east over the Columbia River. The ride follows moderately graded old roads except for the first and last mile, which are on a paved road. Portions of the return trip are along a different route, so you'll be able to experience more of the area.

VARIATIONS: You have the option of taking a 0.4-mile round–trip side spur to a small summit. To save about 2.5 miles round trip you could begin from a parking area farther along the route.

Take Washington 14 for 6.9 miles west of the Bridge of the Gods, which is accessible from I-84 at Cascade Locks, or 28.4 miles west of the I-205 Bridge to the unofficial parking area on the west side of Beacon Rock.

Ride on the paved road that heads north from Washington 14 just west of the Beacon Rock State Park headquarters building. One hundred feet beyond the 1.0 mile marker stay right on unpaved CG 1401, following signs pointing to Equestrian Trailhead, which is the optional place to begin the ride. Mountain bikers always need to be considerate of others who are sharing the route and they must be particularly so around horses. Never go fast by them and, if necessary, walk your bike or even just stop.

At 2.7 miles stay straight on the main (middle) road, farther on head downhill and at 3.7 miles pass where the westerly loop trail on Hamilton Mountain (No. 36) meets the road. Two-tenths mile farther where the road forks, stay straight. You will be returning down the main road that curves to the right here.

At 5.4 miles where a road comes in on the right stay straight (left) and 0.1 mile farther turn right and follow along a crest. At 5.7 miles come to that 0.2 mile, rocky spur that heads to the small summit. To continue the ride, stay left and begin about a mile-long fun, easy downhill run, staying straight where a road comes in on the right. You'll want to linger on the broad crest and savor the scene. Turn right, curve to the left in a short distance and descend in long switchbacks on a road with a somewhat loose gravel cover to the junction with the road you took in. Remember to watch out for hikers along the road down from the saddle because it is part of that Hamilton Mountain Trail loop.

Hamilton Mountain Loop

L ike Dog Mountain (No. 38) to the east, Hamilton Mountain lures hikers back for many return visits. One reason, aside from the fact that it's a fun, scenically varied trail, is that on clear days in late fall through early spring, when the routes on the south side of the Gorge mostly are in shade, Hamilton Mountain basks in the sun.

36

HIKE
DISTANCE: 8 miles round trip
ELEVATION GAIN: 2,200 feet round trip
HIGH POINT: 2,445 feet
ALLOW: 4 1/2 hours round trip
USUALLY OPEN: March through November

VARIATIONS: Although the trip can be shortened by 1.5 miles by taking the direct route up and back and not making the loop, hikers are encouraged to do the circuit because of the superb views up the Columbia River as they travel along the summit ridge. Following the original trail, the eastern leg of the possible loop, just to Little Hamilton Mountain is a fine choice for those who want an shorter hike in both distance and elevation gain. The round trip to this area would be 4.4 miles with 1,580 feet of uphill.

Take Washington 14 for 6.9 miles west of the Bridge of the Gods, which is accessible from I-84 at Cascade Locks, or 28.4 miles east of the I-205 Bridge and turn north onto the road across from Beacon Rock (No. 34). Drive uphill 0.6 mile to a large parking area on the right. The trail begins from the north side behind the restrooms.

Head east and curve into a large basin, staying straight on the main trail where two paths head off on the left. After an open stretch

Hikers above clouds on Little Hamilton Mountain with Nesmith Point in background.

reenter woods and at about 1.2 miles pass a 100-foot-long spur to a view into the canyon holding Rodney Creek. At the next junction turn left to reach Pool of the Winds, a rock walled chamber at Rodney Falls.

The main trail switchbacks down from the junction of the spur to the Pool to the bridge over Rodney Creek and then winds up to the junction of a 100-yard path to the top of Hardy Falls. The main route continues up in six switchbacks to a fork at 1.6 miles, the lower end of the possible loop.

You can make the circuit either way, but it is described here in a clockwise direction. Stay left, traverse through a slope of mostly deciduous trees to a road, turn right and after 200 yards come to a fork and curve right on the main road. The road that continues straight is the route of No. 35. Follow the road up for 0.8 mile to a broad, open ridge crest with views of Table (No. 37), Dog and Wind Mountains, Beacon Rock and Mt. Hood. Walk south along the crest to an obvious trail that traverses along the west side of the slope and eventually returns to the crest. Where you come to the junction of the upper end of the easterly route, stay left and walk several yards to the bush-surrounded summit from which you can see Mounts Adams and St. Helens and down onto Bonneville Dam.

From the junction just before the summit the main trail winds down mostly open slopes in tight switchbacks to the impressive rock faces of Little Hamilton Mountain and then continues down in woods to the junction with the lower end of the loop.

Rodney Falls.

Rock below Rodney Falls.

Bonneville Dam from Little Hamilton Mountain.

Table Mountain

37

HIKE
DISTANCE: 14 miles round trip
ELEVATION GAIN: 3,700 feet round trip
HIGH POINT: 3,300 feet
ALLOW: 8 hours round trip
USUALLY OPEN: May through November

Looking south from the Pacific Crest Trail to Table Mountain with Mt. Hood in background.

Climbing the steep slope of what remains of Table Mountain's south face, after it and a portion of Greenleaf Peak slid into the Columbia River to form the legendary Bridge of the Gods, to the aptly named long summit is a measure of a hiker's conditioning. You'll travel through a variety of scenery and from the summit have views that extend from Larch Mountain past other Gorge landmarks to Mt. Defiance, Mt. Hood and, to the north, mounts St. Helens, Rainier and Adams.

A few times the lower part of the route makes little joggles at old road crossings and a pipeline, but, because you will be on the Pacific Crest Trail, staying on course should be no problem. Shorter ways exist to reach Table Mountain, but they begin on private property.

VARIATIONS: Those wanting a shorter hike of 11 miles round trip with 1,500 feet of gentle to moderate uphill can go to Aldrich Butte, which, although considerably lower than Table Mountain, also provides a fine, far-ranging view. Wildflowers are especially delightful here from late May through early June. Two return loops from the summit of Table Mountain are possible for experienced hikers.

Take Washington 14 to a large trailhead parking area off the north side of the road between the 39 and 40 mile posts. This is 2.0 miles west of the north end of the Bridge of the Gods.

Take the signed Tamanous Trail and after 0.5 mile meet the PCT, which began its Washington section just west of the Bridge of the Gods, and turn left. Follow the PCT past a variety of terrain, including two lakes and some rocky areas.

At 4.3 and 4.5 miles cross and recross an old road. Variations are possible here, but the most straightforward route is to continue on the PCT. About 0.5 mile farther be on the lookout for a probably unsigned trail heading up to the right. Continue on the PCT for another 0.5 mile to a second intersection, turn right here and begin the steep uphill. You'll be distracted from your labors by much open, rocky terrain. A loop has been possible from the east side of the summit area and its lower end is the path you passed 0.5 mile before the one you took up. However,

Table Mountain at sunset.

the upper portion of this easterly route is rubble strewn and sometimes faint. Hikers also can go to the northwest corner of the summit and take a narrow little use dpath down to a road. Follow it to a junction, turn left and take that road down to where the PCT crosses.

To reach Aldrich Butte here are your landmarks: At about

Bonneville Dam from Aldrich Butte.

2.0 miles travel above a second, smaller small lake and then cross Greenleaf Creek on a bridge. About 0.5 mile farther come to an old road and turn left. If you cross a second bridge, you will need to backtrack. Come to a fork at the north end of Carpenters Marsh. Turn right and after about 200 yards veer left onto a road and follow it up about 0.5 mile to the summit.

Cliff below summit of Table Mountain with Mt. Hood in background.

Dog Mountain

HIKE

38

DISTANCE: 6.0 miles round trip
ELEVATION GAIN: 2,900 feet round trip
HIGH POINT: 2,948 feet
ALLOW: 4 to 4 1/2 hours round trip
USUALLY OPEN: March through December

Dog Mountain is easily one of the most popular hikes in the Gorge and the reasons are plentiful: Around mid-May the vast, open summit area is densely covered with the big yellow blooms of balsamroot; three separate, interconnecting trails afford hikers many options for loops; the middle of those three, being the most direct, is a favorite of people wanting an efficient workout along with their hiking fun; on a clear day from late fall through early spring, Dog Mountain's trails will be in the sun, unlike most of the routes on the Oregon side.

Note that Dog Mountain is the most westerly of the trails on the Washington side where you might encounter rattlesnakes.

VARIATIONS: Any route on Dog Mountain is superb, but the combination offering the most views is to take the westerly, longest trail up and return along the easterly one.

Ice-coated trees on Dog Mountain.

A trail to Augsperger Mountain, the larger peak behind Dog Mountain to the northeast, branches off from the westerly route and taking it at some time definitely is recommended. One open slope along the climb affords good views and the woods near the summit have a distinctly alpine ambiance. The hike is about 16 miles round trip with approximately 4,100 feet of elevation gain.

Coming from the west, drive on Washington 14 for 12.8 miles east of the Bridge of the Gods, which is accessible from I-84 at Cascade Locks, to a huge parking area off the north side of the road. Approaching from the east, drive about 18 miles west of the Hood River Bridge. The westerly trail begins from near the northeast end of the parking area and initially climbs to the west. About three-quarters of the way up stay right at the junction of the trail to Augsperger Mountain and continue climbing to the west end of the summit loop. If you stay left you'll have an open stretch and then a section through woods. Both branches come together at the junction with the middle and easterly trails, which are concurrent here, at Puppy Mountain, the

Trail through field of balsamroot on upper Dog Mountain.

little bench where fire lookout buildings once stood.

If you want to take the middle or easterly route up, head east from the parking area on an old road bed for about 300 feet then turn left and begin climbing along slopes that support many wildflowers in spring. Come to a bench where the trails diverge. They rejoin about 0.3 mile below the start of the open summit area. Where you come to the bottom end of the summit loop at Puppy Mountain, it's suggested you stay right and do the circuit in a counterclockwise direction.

From the open slopes you look directly across to Starvation Ridge and Mt. Defiance (No. 24), easily identified by the tall towers. As you begin descending along the summit loop, you'll also have an excellent perspective of Mt. St. Helens.

Historic photo of the former fire lookout on Dog Mountain with Mt. Defiance in background.

Nestor Peak

39

BIKE	HIKE
DISTANCE: 13.2 miles round trip	**DISTANCE:** 8 miles round trip
ELEVATION GAIN: 2,800 feet round trip	**ELEVATION GAIN:** 2,100 feet round trip
HIGH POINT: 3,088 feet	**ALLOW:** 3 1/2 hours round trip
ALLOW: 3 1/2 to 4 hours round trip	
USUALLY OPEN: April through November	

You can reach the summit of Nestor Peak with its views across the Columbia River to the Lower Hood River Valley, features in the Gorge and landmarks considerably more distant, either on a mountain bike along unpaved roads or by foot on trails and roads. As with most outings at the east end of the Gorge, the region is at its best in spring and autumn.

For bikers, except for the final few hundred feet, the road grades are moderate and the surfaces good, although some sections will be slippery when wet. Watch out for rattlesnakes.

Drive on Washington 14 for 22.3 miles east of the Bridge of the Gods or 1.5 miles west of the Hood River Bridge to junction on the east side of the White Salmon River of State 141 Alternate to Trout Lake. Turn north, after 2.2 miles stay left at the junction of State 141 and continue 2.0 miles to Northwestern Lake Road. Turn left, after 0.4 mile turn left into a park and leave your car here, if you're biking.

Continue on your bicycle along the road for 0.1 to the end of the pavement and stay straight. One-half mile farther turn left on N1000 where a sign points to Buck Creek Trail No. 1 and 1.4 mile farther stay right, continuing on N1000. For much of the ride you'll be traversing wooded slopes but, as is characteristic of the forests this far east in the Gorge, they will be more open and varied. Pass the trailhead for Buck Creek Trail No. 1 after 0.5 mile and at the 2.5-mile point stay left, heading slightly uphill. Two and one-half miles farther, stay right and 0.5 mile farther stay right again on N1600 where a sign points to Nestor Peak. One-tenth mile farther stay left and ride the final mile to the summit. The especially attractive north face of Mt. Hood rises behind the Gorge and Mt. Defiance (No. 24) with its distinctive towers is easy to identify. The view to the north extends over the southernmost Washington Cascades to Mt. Adams.

Fungus on a decayed tree stump.

Mt. Adams from the summit of Nestor Peak.

Hikers can reach the trailhead by following the route given above for the cyclists to the signed trailhead. There is a map of the Buck Creek Trail system at the junction where the pavement ends. A printed map of the entire network can be obtained from the Department of Natural Resources, the address and phone number of which are given on page 80.

Weldon Wagon Trail

40

HIKE/BIKE
DISTANCE: 6.2 miles round trip
ELEVATION GAIN: 1,350 feet round trip
HIGH POINT: 1,800 feet
ALLOW: 3 1/2 hours round trip hiking; 2 hours round trip by bike
USUALLY OPEN: late February through mid-December

Sign at the lower end of the Weldon Wagon Trail.

"Bearing Tree" at the upper end of the Weldon Wagon Trail.

As with the route to Nestor Peak (No. 39), the Weldon Wagon Trail is north of the Gorge proper but it provides views south over terrain there that has no public access. Regardless, the landscape surrounding the old road is most attractive in itself with that pleasing mix of open, grassy slopes and oaks and conifers typical of the area. The route is especially attractive around late April when the wildflowers are at their peaks.

The Weldon Wagon Road, named for one of the two builders, was completed in 1911 and most likely was part of the "apple boom" that occurred in the area during the first two decades of the 1900s.

Parking is so limited that hiking along the unpaved road for the initial few tenths mile is recommended. Be alert for the usual trio in this part of the Gorge: Ticks, poison oak and rattlesnakes.

VARIATION: The average mountain-bike rider will find the upper part of the road portion somewhat rough and the trail sections a bit unnerving. However, those who reach the upper end can make a very fun, mostly downhill loop back along unpaved and paved roads, which would be about 18 miles round trip.

Drive on Washington 14 for 22.3 miles east of the Bridge of the Gods or 1.5 miles west of the Hood River Bridge to the junction on the east side of the White Salmon River of State 141 Alternate to Trout Lake. Turn north, after 2.2 miles stay left at the junction of State 141 and continue north 3.9 miles to Husum. Just beyond the big wooden sign that marks the Weldon Wagon Trail and relates some of its history cross the highway bridge and park off the west side of State 141.

After the first few hundred yards from the sign Indian Creek Road narrows and is lined with more trees. Four-tenths mile from the highway cross a cattle guard and just beyond it stay left at a fork and begin traveling on a dirt, instead of a gravel, surface. After 0.2 mile stay left again and 0.4 mile farther turn right, continuing to follow the signs to Weldon Wagon Trail. In 0.2 mile just as the road begins a little dip look right for the signed trail.

In 0.2 mile leave the deep woods where you merge with the old road bed and have your first views down onto the White Salmon River Valley and beyond to the Hood River Valley to Mt. Hood. Farther on the route narrows to a trail that gently curves around the head of the treeless basin. Reenter deep woods just before the end of the uphill and travel on the level for the last stretch to the Bearing Tree.

If you want to make the loop back continue in the same direction you were riding as you left the woods at the Bearing Tree and come to a wide, unpaved road. Turn right and take it about 3.0 miles to a paved road. Turn right, in about 5.0 miles turn left and then in 0.2 miles turn right. Follow the main route down to State 141, turn right and take it back to your car.

Large oak tree at the edge of the lower forest.

Catherine Creek

HIKE
41

DISTANCE: From 1.0 to 10 miles round trip
ELEVATION GAIN: From 100 to 800 feet round trip
HIGH POINT: Variable
ALLOW: 1/2 hour to 3 hours round trip
USUALLY OPEN: All year except in extreme winter weather

At least for access by the general public, the Catherine Creek area is unique in the Gorge. Nowhere else can you wander about over slopes that are such a perfect blend of open, grassy terrain, mixed forest and rock outcroppings. Like the Sandy River Delta (No. 1), at this time Catherine Creek is classified as a "dispersed recreation site". There are no trail signs nor official routes, although there are many old roads and paths that you can follow. The difference between the Delta area and the Catherine Creek area is that the terrain of the latter, in addition to its less unruly ambiance, makes it considerably easier to stay oriented. And, if you do miscalculate, it's usually little problem to correct your course.

To the south across from the trailhead, however, is a structured, paved loop and you enthusiastically are urged to take this circuit. It winds through a more lush landscape remarkably different from the terrain just across the road. Both areas are noted for their spring wildflowers. The upper part supports a subtle display but this lower section is considerably more rambunctious.

Note that rattlesnakes do inhabit the area, so watch where you walk and sit.

Drive on Washington 14 for 6 miles east of the Hood River Bridge to County Road 1230 just west of mile post 71 and at the west end of Rowland Lake. Yes, on a hot day this lake makes for wonderful swimming. After 1.1 miles pass an old road that is where you will exit if you make the second of the possible trips described below. Come to the parking area for Catherine Creek on the north side of the road 1.5 miles from Washington 14. As noted, you can wander all over the area, but here are two routes to introduce you to the region:

From the parking area follow the faint road that gently descends to the right and then curves left. Cross Catherine Creek and come to an old corral and other ranch buildings. A natural arch is on the wall to the east above the structures. The road continues north to junctions with other roads. Or you could backtrack to the creek and follow the road that travels above its west side.

For the second trip, from the parking area head due north and gently uphill along another old road to a fork. Turn left and soon begin traveling on a path. Farther on traverse downhill on a rocky old road bed to the floor of a little valley. You can turn right and investigate more terrain. If you turn left you will be on the road that goes to the first trailhead noted in the driving directions.

Old corral at Catherine Creek.

Pine and oak forest below the natural arch.

Horsethief Butte

42

HIKE
DISTANCE: 0.5 to 2 miles round trip
ELEVATION GAIN: 100 to 300 or more feet round trip
HIGH POINT: 450 feet
ALLOW: 1/2 to 2 hours round trip
USUALLY OPEN: All year except in severe winter conditions

Looking north from near the summit of Horsethief Butte.

(east), after 1.5 miles pass the entrance to Horsethief Lake State Park and continue on Washington 14 another 1.2 miles to parking off the right shoulder where a sign identifies Horsethief Butte Trail.

After several yards stay straight where a path heads to the right. It traverses in and out of a little canyon and then loops back to Washington 14. Following it is recommended after you complete the big loop. Come to a fork and if you intend to make the circuit turn left (making the loop in a counterclockwise direction is not recommended). You'll be returning on the trail to the right. Where the tread becomes faint continue walking in the same direction until you come to a little ravine from whose edge you'll be able to spot the path that descends from the head of the depression. Follow the path down the floor of the ravine and as you come above a marshy area look across it for the obvious route that climbs from the opposite side. At the bench at the top of that uphill find another easy route up to another bench. From it head toward the base of the face of Horsethief Butte and intercept an obvious trail.

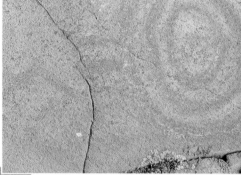

Indian pictograph near Horsethief Butte.

From a distance, Horsethief Butte, on the Washington side of the Gorge east of The Dalles, appears to be one big mass of rock. In fact, the interior is a delightful warren of little canyons and gullies. An added diversion for hikers is the probability of observing rock climbers. Note that the area can be hot in summer and always be on the alert for rattlesnakes, particularly from late spring through early fall. Although visitors can confine themselves to trails, the recommended itinerary, which involves easy cross-country and route finding, is to circumnavigate Horsethief Butte.

VARIATIONS: The bench of open, level terrain to the north of Horsethief Butte's base invites unstructured exploring. More adventuresome types could work their ways up to the summit of Horsethief Butte. Also, you could explore nearby Horsethief Lake State Park.

If you're approaching from the Oregon side take I-84 to The Dalles, cross the Columbia River on the toll free bridge and continue north for 3.1 miles to the junction with Washington 14. Turn right

Indian pictograph near Horsethief Butte.

Turn left and follow this level trail to signs marking the path up into Horsethief Butte and climb to the "main room". If you investigate any of the "hallways" to other rooms, you'll want to take the easiest way up. Be sure to note landmarks so you also take the same easy way back.

After you explore the interior descend to the junction with that level, main trail and continue your loop around to the fork near the start of the hike.

Resources

Most of the public lands of the Columbia River Gorge are under the management of the Columbia River Gorge National Scenic Area. However, other agencies do have jurisdiction over some places. If you have questions or comments, contact the appropriate agency. Their addresses follow with hike numbers appropriate to each:

COLUMBIA RIVER GORGE NATIONAL SCENIC AREA
902 Wasco Suite 200
Hood River, OR 97031
541/386-2333
Open weekdays 7:30 to 4:30
1, 3, 4, 5, 6, 7, 8, 9, 10, 11, 13, 14, 16, 17, 18, 19, 20, 21, 22, 23, 24, 25, 37, 38, 41

ROOSTER ROCK STATE PARK
P.O. Box 100
Corbett, OR 97019
2, 12, 23, 24

OREGON DEPARTMENT OF TRANSPORTATION
123 N.W. Flanders
Portland, OR 97209
503/731-8200
15, 30

HOOD RIVER RANGER DISTRICT
Mt. Hood National Forest
6780 Highway 35
Parkdale, OR 97041
541/352-6002
26, 27, 28, 29
Also the portions of all trails that are within the Mark O. Hatfield Wilderness:
16, 17, 18, 19, 20, 21, 22, 24, 29

THE NATURE CONSERVANCY
821 S.E. 14th Ave.
Portland, OR 97214
503/230-1221
32

DESCHUTES STATE PARK
89600 Biggs-Rufus Highway
Wasco, OR 97065
541/739-2322
33

BEACON ROCK STATE PARK
34841 State Road 14
Skamania, WA 98648
509/427-8265
34, 35, 36

WASHINGTON DEPARTMENT OF NATURAL RESOURCES; SOUTHEAST REGION
713 E. Bowers Road
Ellensburg, WA 98926-9341
509/925-8510
39

KLICKITAT COUNTY PATHS AND TRAILS PROGRAM
228 NW 2nd Street
Goldendale, WA 98620
509/773-4616
40

BUREAU OF LAND MANAGEMENT
1103 N. Fancher
Spokane, WA 99212
509/536-1200
42

Vista House on Crown Point from the east.